TWO DOGS & A GARDEN

Dr. Derelie Cherry, PhD (Univ. Sydney)
Although she worked in publishing for twenty years, commissioning books by Australian authors such as Allan Seale, Sarah Guest and Simon Griffiths, Mary Moody and Clive Blazey, and gained a doctorate in history, all Derelie ever really wanted was two dogs and a garden. She never envisaged a husband in this picture — at least, not until she met Bob Cherry at the Melbourne International Flower Show in 1999. This book tells the story of her life since coming to live in Bob's Paradise.

Matilda poppies, bred by Bob.

In Memory of Trudy – my constant companion and brave little heart.

Trudy watching over us in Paradise.

Published by
Paradise Publishers
147 Greta Road
Kulnura, NSW 2250
Australia
Ph: +61 02 43761403
www.twodogsandagarden.com

Text and Photographs © Derelie Cherry 2009
Reprinted 2009

All rights reserved. No part of this publication may be reproduced, stored in or introduced into a retrieval system, or transmitted in any form or by any means (electronic, mechanical, photocopying, recording or otherwise) without the prior written permission of the publisher.

National Library of Australia
Cataloguing-in-Publication entry

Author: Cherry, Derelie Ann
Title: Two dogs & a garden / Derelie Cherry.
ISBN 9780646509570 (hbk.)
Notes: Includes index.
Subjects: Cherry, Derelie Ann
   Cherry, Bob.
   Gardeners–New South Wales–Kulnura–Biography.
   Plant breeders–New South Wales–Kulnura–Biography.
   Rural landowners–New South Wales–Kulnura–Biography.

Dewey Number: 635.092

Designer Diane Quick
Editor Catherine Page
Printer Everbest Printing, China

Cover French roses such as the glowing apricot/watermelon 'Emilien Guillot' and the pale pink 'Chantal Merieux' are amongst my special favourites.
Pages 2–3 Our bridge is not quite like Monet's water lily bridge at Giverny but Bob plans to eventually have a similar one further down the garden.
Page 13 Camellia pitardii var. *pitardii* always has a mass of blooms in season.
Page 35 Masses of *Camellia* hybrid 'Paradise Illumination' to choose from in the nursery.
Page 47 A section of our *Wisteria* wall illuminated by the setting sun.
Page 63 Trudy thinks that these walls were made especially for her.
Page 79 The moist temperate forests in China are unbelievably beautiful.
Page 95 Our double pink May bush looks so enchanting in spring.
Page 109 The pumpkin patch at Paradise has spread out all over this slope.
Page 119 Various wattles flower in succession throughout the whole year.
Page 133 Amaryllis belladonna has a very aristocratic air about it.
Page 145 The row of 'Simply Magic' that we pass on our daily walk.
Page 183 Delicate pale blue *Plumbago* petals remind me of the finest silk.
Page 199 The gum trees on Bunny Hill have the most splendid bark at Christmas.
Page 219 Fraxinus creticum almost glows in our autumn landscape.

Contents

Foreword 8
Our Paradise 11
The Story of the Camellia 13
A Nursery on Our Doorstep 35
Sensational Scents 47
The Follies of Bob 63
Botanising with Bob 79
Spring Blossom 95
Fresh from the Garden 109
On the Wild Side 119
Flowers Fantastic 133
A Bucket of Roses 145
Colour Parade 185
On Bunny Hill 201
Autumn Gold 221
Acknowledgements 235
Index 237

Foreword

It was at a dinner in the Royal Botanic Gardens in Sydney that I first heard the name Bob Cherry. The then Director of the Gardens, Professor Carrick Chambers, told me of an extraordinary garden up the Pacific Highway between Sydney and Newcastle and of the remarkable chap who ran it, one Bob Cherry. Never shy about cold-calling a perfect stranger, I telephoned Bob and asked if I might visit. Little the professor had told me prepared me for the amazing spectacle that awaited me at the aptly named Paradise Plants, in – I kid you not – Cherry Lane, Kulnura, where Bob has his commercial nursery and the spectacular contiguous private garden that spills out on all sides from the modest house where he and Derelie live. Arcades, walled gardens, paths hemmed in with absurdly floriferous roses, garden pavilions, torrents of camellias, rhododendrons and an almost unimaginable array of magnolias. A horticultural Valhalla. Bob is a plant hunter in the great Victorian tradition, going where few have gone before, mainly throughout Asia but further afield as well, and returning with the rarest of material. He grows it all on and selects particular specimens for commercial propagation, the income from the nursery fuelling his wanderlust, his pursuit of the rare and his almost Ludwigian desire to build. He is supported in this enterprise by his wife Derelie, who is equally passionate about plants and flowers and the author of this record of a unique garden. It could not have been more lovingly chronicled.

    I have many memories of visits to Kulnura but perhaps the most magical was one warm summer afternoon when I took the noted Melbourne gardener Michael McCoy up to meet Bob. We ooh'ed and aah'ed our way around the garden with Bob giving us cuttings of everything we admired. That is his generous habit. Indeed every time he came upon a treasure on his travels he kept one and presented another to the Botanic Gardens. At the end of our walk we felt we had sensual overload. But there was more. We came upon a large dam in which Bob, rather than regard it as a mere water supply, had planted hundreds of lotus. They were in full fantastic bloom and in a small boat we floated among them, their huge flower heads as high as the sides of the boat and no sound but the bush birds and the gentle lap of water. Paradise indeed.

Leo Schofield

In our climate each bloom of 'Molineux' has subtle variations in colour.

Bob took advantage of one fine autumn day to soar into the air in a tiny plane and take some photographs.

Our Paradise

Our 92 hectares of Paradise, located one hour north of Sydney, are set in the picturesque sandstone hinterland of the Central Coast. Surrounded by rugged gorges and lush coastal valleys, the plateau on which we are perched 33 degrees south of the equator, is 300 metres above sea level, and Bob is convinced there is always a patch of blue in the sky directly above us. Our annual rainfall is around 1036 mm, although our recent years of drought saw nothing like this. Plants thrive in our temperate humid climate, which makes it the perfect place for Paradise.

Open Weekends

The garden in Paradise is open to the public each year on the first weekend in May (autumn), the first weekend in August (spring) and the last weekend in October (roses).

The enormous sprays of *C. reticulata* 'Temple Mist' have to be navigated around when strolling down this pathway near the house.

The Story of the Camellia

< Our grove of *Camellia reticulata* 'Chuxiong Gold', which we constantly check for any variation in the blooms.

According to Bob

Once upon a time, about 5000 years ago, people began to change their lifestyles. Where previously they had practiced hunting and gathering to survive, now they started to form agricultural communities. Before long, groups developed within these societies, including classes of artisans, merchants, priests and others who had the time and leisure to make a garden.

The use of camellias in medicine and beverages has been recorded for the last 3000 years in China, and camellia oil is still widely used throughout Asia today for cooking and manufacturing cosmetics. *Camellia sinensis* was first described in China in the 5th Century BC as a "tea-vegetable", because its leaves were boiled and steamed and then compressed into blocks to eat as a pickled vegetable.

Bob believes that camellias were useful to people even longer ago than 5000 years. But, as societies developed, and interest in gardening emerged, how did camellias evolve? Well, it all goes back to variation in the species growing in the wild. Not only sports on the same plant, but entirely different plants. Imagine, one day, the priest spotting

v The extremely elegant *C. reticulata* 'Purple Gown' has been growing in China for hundreds of years.

< Camellias surround a lake at a resort near Guilin, in China's Guangxi province.

a bright double pink *C. japonica* amongst the mostly single red blooms in the wild. Or maybe a single white *C. reticulata* growing amongst the wild groves of mostly pink to red single blooms. With a chance of only one in 10,000, or even only one in 100,000, flowers could vary in either size of bloom, colour or number of petals. Naturally, anyone interested would want this rarity, which would then be grown and reproduced by the wealthier classes. And as time passed and gardens became larger, these collections of plants of various colours and forms led to even greater variability through cross-pollination.

∧ Trudy amongst the blooms of *C.* hybrid 'Contemplation'.

> On our open weekends in Paradise we display the versatility of the *Camellia*.

It is only since the 18th century that great gardens have been created in the western world. Merchants and plant collectors brought back many different forms of camellias from China and Japan, both species and cultivars, and introduced them to nurseries and gardens. The last fifty years have seen tremendous advances in breeding camellias. Today there is an enormous diversity in form, colour and size. In 1916 only thirty-eight Camellia species had been discovered; by 1954 there were eighty-two species; but today there are around 350 species. In Paradise we grow about eighty of these, a substantial proportion indeed for a private garden.

∧ Part of our *C. sinensis* tea plantation.

Bob's wanderlust, especially throughout China, has led him to many wonderful encounters while hunting for camellias. One story that I always like to hear is how he acquired *C. japonica* 'Incarnata', an exquisite formal double *Camellia* with incurved petals in a delicate shade of pink, sometimes with touches of white. On this occasion the mayor of Jinhua was delighted that a group of westerners were visiting his town, in southern China, for the very first time. Bob was amongst a group of *Camellia* enthusiasts who were welcomed as celebrities by the local dignitaries. Speech after speech was made during the formal opening of

A Camellia 2000 Years Old

the *Camellia* show and the next day Bob was given a plant in a pot that the mayor told him had been growing in his town for over 2000 years! When we travelled to the Azores a few years ago with some fellow enthusiasts, we were delighted to discover dark pink, white and red versions of this same *Camellia*.

There are numerous examples of other individual *Camellia* plants, over 500 years old, that Bob has seen growing in temples throughout China. He relates another particularly exciting story about a visit to the small village of Chuxiong in south-western China, there he came across the striking large red flowered *C. reticulata* 'Chuxiong Gold'. The local villagers gathered around and, much to his amazement, Bob was informed that about fifty years ago, one red flower, with an unusual gold edge, had bloomed on the plant. This was direct evidence of his theory of variation. We have several trees of this *Camellia* growing in our garden, and we regularly check them for any variation. Just imagine our excitement if we discovered a bloom with a golden edge!

C. japonica 'Incarnata', which has been growing in China for 2000 years.

It is not surprising that *C.* hybrid 'Water Lily' is so similar to 'Dream Boat'; the seed for both came from the same seed pod.

Breeding Camellia sasanqua

I first came across *Camellia sasanqua* when I lived in Kirribilli Avenue in Sydney. At the end of this lovely avenue are the magnificent stone residences of the Prime Minister and the Governor General. And in May every year, the footpaths outside these houses were covered in a pale pink carpet of delicate blossom. I soon discovered that the flowers were not suitable for picking as they shattered so quickly. But for a street display, these small trees were hard to surpass.

C. sasanqua, which originated in Japan, is a relative newcomer to Australia and the rest of the world. In fact, the first cultivated plant was recorded in France as recently as 1869. But plant collectors of old were mostly from Europe, and they were only interested in collecting plants that would grow in their home regions. So the rest of the world had to wait. Most of the camellias available in Australia until the 1950s were *C. japonica*. In the 1920s there were a few *C. sasanqua* and there was just one *C. reticulata*, 'Captain Rawes', which was imported into Australia from China in 1860.

C. hybrid 'Dream Boat', bred in New Zealand, is almost lavender pink with darker edges on the petals.

\> The *C. sasanqua* 'Red Willow' trees planted around our swimming pool are so picturesque amongst the autumn colour.

∧ Statues, such as this lovely Italian bronze face, perfectly complement the *Camellia* flower.

> *C. sasanqua* 'Paradise Sayaka' is one of our loveliest cultivars and has a definite oriental look about it.

In the 1960s there were only about thirty *C. sasanqua* cultivars available in Australia, and Bob acquired all that he possibly could. He observed that the only types of *C. sasanqua* available commercially had white or pale pink flowers that were quite small, and that there were very few reds. Furthermore, in the wild, *C. sasanqua* flowers were even smaller and mostly white, sometimes pink, but never red. Equally important, Bob noted that these plants possessed sought-after qualities such as early flowering, rapid growth and resistance to disease. So he took up the gauntlet and set about establishing his breeding programme in the 1980s, specifically focusing on developing different characteristics in the flowers of the *C. sasanqua*, as well as a sturdy growth habit.

His programme rapidly expanded in the ensuing years, until 3000 hand-pollinated crosses were carried out annually at Paradise. From these, only about 1000 seeds set, and from these again, only about three were good enough to release on the market. Even then, it took another four years or more before they were commercially available. All in all, there is about a seven-year gestation period from first sighting.

∧ *C. sasanqua* 'Paradise Pearl' has an ethereal quality.

> *C. japonica* 'Roma Risorta' was bred in Rome in 1866. The unusual carmine streaks enhance its overall beauty.

The pattern on the petals of *C. japonica* 'R. L. Wheeler Variegated' is actually caused by a virus.

Camellias All Year Round

∧ *C. changii*, also known as *C. azalea*, blooms all year round.

"How would you like a *Camellia* that blooms midsummer as well as in winter?" Bob asked me one day. "We're working on getting one," he announced. A relatively new species, *C. changii* (also known as *C. azalea*) could be the key to this. Its vivid orange-red flowers, up to 125 mm in diameter, grow on an attractive compact plant that has thick leathery leaves with a blue reverse. It was only recently discovered in the tropical Chinese province of Guangdong, and it blooms all year round.

During the season, Bob looks for new babies each morning among the potted-up new plants, which are spread out on black plastic underneath shady trees. Just the other day he pointed out one very promising-looking bud – like 'Paradise Belinda', hot pink and large. And another one that I thought was lovely – bright pink, like the rosette-shaped 'Paradise Petite', but with more petals.

" a Camellia that resembles cherry blossom? "

> One of Bob's beautiful, unnamed seedlings.

Naming these new babies is always fun. On one occasion, when the Vaucluse Garden Club was visiting, we took the members over to see what was new that day. To our surprise, a beautiful large white-flushed pink flower with many central stamens had come out overnight. Of course, I thought it should be called 'Paradise Vaucluse'. It is wonderfully exciting to see how Bob's plans are unfolding. Some treasures for the future include a superb range of true red *C. sasanqua*, a curved formal miniature, a frilly pink-flowered specimen to be called 'Paradise Little Miss E' (after my maiden name, Evely), and one with a low spreading growth habit, called 'Paradise Regina', which has the loveliest lavender to dusky pink flowers. And I couldn't forget the new double pink that is to be named after me.

Good colour, and lots of it, is the most sought-after characteristic of all. Some of Bob's crosses have resulted in perfectly shaped blooms, in the most delectable shade of pink, that extend right along the stem. Camellias that flower in this fashion are entirely new, and very exciting. And a *Camellia* that resembles cherry blossom? Well, Bob sees that in the future too. By crossing *C. longipedicellata*, whose flowers hang down in long pedicels, with a small cluster-flowered hybrid, it could be achievable.

For Bob, camellias are the most attractive and versatile of all garden plants. In Paradise we have forests of camellias, hedges of camellias in all shapes and sizes, specimen plants, beds of just camellias, and others mixed beds. They can be espaliered up walls, used in pleached hedges, grown as groundcovers, or even in hanging baskets. Most significantly, they grow in full sun or shade and everything in between. Only in areas of bad frost do they prefer some shelter, to prevent the flowers turning brown.

Bob's Choice Camellias

> Our grove of mainly pink and white *C. sasanqua*, near the house, is a visual delight.

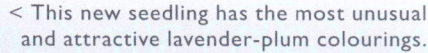
< This new seedling has the most unusual and attractive lavender-plum colourings.

The tranquil *C. sasanqua* forest, near the house, is one of our favourite groves of camellias in the garden. Every May the ground is carpeted with pink and white blossom from sixty *C. sasanqua* trees that are thirty-five years old and four metres tall. Bob has created a canopy by chopping off all the lower branches up to a height of about two metres, and to walk beneath these small trees is pure magic! Clumps of tiny mauve-pink cyclamens, scattered here and there, add to the enchantment. I had always thought this forest was made up of mostly the same variety. But when I asked Bob recently what they were, he surprised me with his reply: "There's a mixture, including 'Plantation Pink', 'Exquisite', 'Kanjiro', 'Rosea', 'Red Willow' and 'Violet Weymouth'."

Immediately in front of the house, edging the footpath and growing under eleven trident maple trees that are now 20 metres tall, Bob planted ten bushes of the low-growing *C. sasanqua* 'Shishigashira'. They have made a lovely bushy hedge of crimson pink blooms. And just along the path, *C. sasanqua* 'Sparkling Burgundy' forms a five-metre-high hedge that puts on a spectacular show each year. Towards the back of the house is another four-metre-high hedge of *C. williamsii* 'Wynne Raynor'. The clear-pink blooms are mostly semi-double but some have an anemone centre. Simply superb.

One of Bob's favourite species is *C. amplexicaulis*.

^ A new *Camellia* hybrid, bred by Bob, to be called 'Little Miss E'.

It is most unusual, with large waxy flowers and big shiny leaves. In the wild, near Tam Dao in northern Vietnam, it varies in colour from white, through pink, to red shades. And Bob's collection of yellow species is the best in Australia. He has even built a special tunnel shadehouse for them, covered with heavy-duty weed mat to replicate their growing conditions in the dense tropical forests of North Vietnam and south-east China.

∧ Our new 'Paradise Regina' will make a lovely low-growing hedge with its lavender-pink blooms.

< Some more of Bob's gorgeous new *Camellia* hybrid seedlings.

∧ This new cluster-flowered hybrid is especially exciting.

∧ Bob is stunned by the luscious huge blooms of *C. reticulata* 'Raspberry Glow', which was bred in New Zealand by Harry Cave.

∧ *C. sasanqua* 'Paradise Petite' is so popular because of its small leaves and dainty rosette-type flowers.

∧ This hedge is one of the best in our garden. It is made up of *C. sasanqua* 'Shishigashira', which is a Japanese variety that is over one hundred years old.

> Another of Bob's unnamed seedlings that shows great promise.

Bob includes what he calls 'the girls' amongst his favourites: *C. sasanqua* x *C. reticulata* 'Flower Girl', 'Show Girl' and 'Dream Girl'. Long flowering, in the most pleasing shades of pink, they have an extended flowering season with lots of blooms. Spread throughout the garden, they brighten up many corners with their dramatic appearance, although clusters of them planted together are just as effective.

Bob's philosophy is that plant breeders have a responsibility to create beauty. Especially beauty that lasts as long as possible – so extending the flowering season is of vital importance. Leaving his imprint on the world through plants for future generations gives Bob immense satisfaction. He would love to return in a few hundred years, as he is sure he would find some of his best *C. sasanqua* cultivars still growing and treasured.

It was because of camellias that Bob and I met. I had read about a large garden, with over 1000 camellias, that was north of Sydney and about to have its first open weekend. Doug Haviland, then Secretary of the NSW Camellia Research Society, well remembers our conversation at that time. So in August 1996 I made my first journey up to Paradise. I had no idea who owned the garden, but I remember thinking that whoever it was, I liked their style. And when I discovered a row of my favourite pink *Dianthus* planted all along one long bed, I almost thought they had been planted especially for me! I sat down on the grassy bank beside the huge lake and contemplated the meaning of life for over two hours. Today Bob loves to say "She sat down right outside my bedroom window!" Not only was that so, even though I had no idea, but I even entered his house on that first occasion. I was hungry and thought it was a restaurant. Not surprising really, for the front door was wide open. So I wandered in, but there were no chairs and tables

A Garden with 1000 Camellias

∧ Enormous trees of *C.* hybrid 'Flower Girl' (front) and 'Show Girl' at the bottom of our garden are real show-stoppers.

< The blooms on the *C.* hybrid 'Flower Girl' have a beautiful colour and formation.

^ On a recent trip to the province of Szechuan in China, we were invited to assist in official celebrations to plant a new hillside *Camellia* garden. My *Camellia* was called 'Eighteen Scholars' and it is an astounding variety that has blooms in eighteen different colours on the one plant.

Serendipity

to be seen. Instead sparse furniture was dotted here and there. Suddenly the thought entered my mind "I have a funny feeling that someone lives here – I think I had better get out!"

Down the bottom of the garden that same day, I came across the largest, most glorious pink *Camellia* flowers I had ever seen. Four huge trees were smothered in these stupendous blooms. I clearly recall standing in front of them and thinking that if these fantastic specimens grew at the bottom of my garden, I would live happily forever after. They were *C. reticulata* 'Lasca Beauty'. Little did I ever dream that day that several years later I would travel in China with not only the owner of this garden but also the breeder of 'Lasca Beauty', Dr Clifford Parks, who lives in America.

Only a few years later, I encountered the magnificent blooms of another *C. reticulata* that also inspired me. I was having lunch with the much-loved and admired Australian media personality, Allan Seale, to discuss what turned out to be his last of twenty books, *New Life for Old Gardens*. As I left his house I admired some stunning large red camellias growing on bushes planted either side of his front door. "Would you like to take some with you?" he suggested. The gasps of awe back in the office, where they sat on my desk later that afternoon, did not stop for the rest of the day! I think those blooms were probably the stunning frilly *C. reticulata* 'Dr Clifford Parks'.

Bob and I were not destined to meet until three years later. But on that first auspicious visit of mine to Paradise, fate was already working overtime. On my arrival I had noticed beautiful bunches of poppies for sale when I walked down to the garden through the nursery. They were in glorious pale shades of pink, red, white, apricot and lemon, as well as the

> Our large hedge of *C. sasanqua* 'Sparkling Burgundy'

∧ Some very beautiful camellias have been bred in New Zealand, including the lovely soft pink *C. pitardii* x *C. japonica* 'Contemplation'.

Trudy and Jessee wait patiently while their Mum takes yet more *Camellia* photographs.

∧ The enormous blooms of
C. reticulata 'Lasca Beauty' can be
almost as big as dinner plates.

more common brighter yellow and orange shades, and I was later to learn that they were the 'Matilda' poppies, bred by Bob. But when I returned in the afternoon to buy some, all the pale shades had gone. Someone said, "If you go down to the poppy patch, you can probably pick your own." Several young girls were amongst the one hectare field of poppies, picking more to sell. I explained to the eldest what I was after and she generously replied, "Help yourself." These days she is my eldest step-daughter, Jennifer, and the other two girls were her sisters, Louise and Caroline. Jenny can still recall my visit, and she told her father later that same day, "We found a nice lady for you, Dad." To which Bob apparently replied, "Well, where is she?"

The following year, in May 1997, I returned once again to Paradise, this time bringing a girlfriend with me. Meg encountered an old friend from university days who was selling plants in the top tent, and I asked him who owned this incredible place. Peter replied: "His name is Bob Cherry, but he's hardly ever here. He travels in China a lot."

It was at the Melbourne International Flower Show in 1999 that Bob and I finally met. I had appointments with some of my authors and planned to check out gardening trends as well. My Thursday lunch engagement was with Clive Blazey from the Digger's Club, but prior to that, I had plenty of time to look around the exhibits. When I accidentally came across a stand for 'Paradise Plants', I wondered if, by chance, the elusive Bob Cherry would be there. Because he had the reputation of being the leading *Camellia* expert in Australia, perhaps one day there could be a book. As fate would have it, Bob turned out to be the first person I spoke to on the stand. Within 24 hours he had told a colleague that he had met the person he was going to marry.

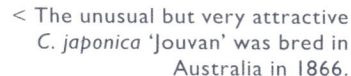

< The unusual but very attractive
C. japonica 'Jouvan' was bred in
Australia in 1866.

BOB'S GOLDEN RULES FOR GROWING CAMELLIAS

PREPARE the soil well, adding well-rotted manure or compost. A little time and effort spent on enriching the soil will result in a bigger plant more quickly.

WATER around the base of the stem at least twice a week for 3–4 months after planting, until new roots grow out of the old root ball into the surrounding soil.

FEED once a year, preferably in September, with any mixed fertiliser such as camellia and azalea food, although rose and citrus food is just as good. In pots, use a slow-release fertiliser such as Osmocote.

PRUNE them. Camellias respond well to pruning, and they prefer to be pruned lightly but regularly. However, if you inherit old plants, drastic pruning with a chainsaw is OK. Plants can be pruned to any height required at any time of the year.

All of Bob's sasanquas have been named after family, friends and staff. Here we have, clockwise from left, 'Paradise Jessica', 'Paradise Joy' (two blooms), 'Paradise Elizabeth' and 'Paradise Rebecca'.

Looking across the lake to where we live in the house that Bob built.

What I call our "granny prints" come in the prettiest colour combinations.

A Nursery on Our Doorstep

Thousands on Offer

Like most garden lovers, before I met Bob I visited garden centres and nurseries regularly. So many lovely different plants to choose from, but with space and budget restrictions, it was always difficult. Although I now have a nursery on my doorstep, the problem of choosing remains. But instead of hundreds of plants to select from, there are now thousands. No wonder it takes me a long time to load up yet another wheelbarrow of plants to take down to the garden. And it is so tempting to go back for just another twenty or so. "Now I'm planting out the blue and purple beds," I explain to staff members Joan and Leonie, who laugh as I pass by with my fifth wheelbarrow full of polyanthus.

Granny Prints for Summer

It's only a few days until my birthday on 8 December. I love this time of the year. The roses are coming into their second flush and the hydrangeas, which are my special favourites in the nursery, are in full bloom.

Twice a week, the dogs and I make our selection from the 30,000 hydrangeas that we grow annually. With Christmas coming as well, I brighten up the entrance to the house with pots of them, for instant colour. It is one of my most pleasant tasks. Jenny, who looks after this area in the nursery, inquires "What are you looking for today, Derelie?" "I need a couple of white ones," I reply. Only a few days ago there were lots of whites, but they have gone. "There are a couple somewhere," Jenny tells me as she leads me down the path. "There," she points among the massed blooms, and sure enough she has spotted a couple of superb plants. They are Bob's stock plants. Normally, it would mean hands off, but because they will be near the house, I can take them.

I still cannot decide which are my favourite *Hydrangea* colours. There are shades of amethyst, azure blue, cobalt blue, palest blue and

< This Chinese man, who lives near our front door, looks at home amongst his surroundings.

< Our double hydrangeas are just exquisite.

^ The subtle shades of our doubles make them even more desirable.

< Pots of hydrangeas near the house provide instant colour most effectively.

deep purple, right through to opal and pearl. The rose quartz, bright pink and red are truly spectacular. Perhaps the doubles win first prize from me, but this year they are closely followed by what I call our "granny prints". Just like the material of old that grandma spread on the bed as a coverlet — tiny flower prints in the softest shades — so very pretty and old-fashioned. Especially the white-touched blue ones and the pink-touched mauve.

The day after my birthday I am selling hydrangeas from a stall that I have set up at Cedar Park Lavender Farm down the road in the beautiful Yarramalong Valley. Warwick and Margaret are having their first Open Day and they are giving lavender-distilling demonstrations. Just like in Provence. I like to participate in a few different shows each year because it gives me the opportunity to market-research our plants. Bob does the Nambour Flower Show, in Queensland, with me and he often chats to customers about their likes and dislikes — from colour, to shape and growth habit of the plants. We both observe, with great interest, customers choosing our polyanthus; their choices are often quite the opposite of what we expect.

On this hot, steamy day in December, I set up under a shady tree and await my first customer. "How do you make hydrangeas blue?" is the most popular question of the day. "My Dad used to put old rusty nails in the soil and that turned them a beautiful blue," advises one customer to another. Yes, the acid from iron can help change the colour to blue, but alum is necessary for a really good intense blue. Yet it is interesting that while some whites keep their colour, other whites change colour. Bob tells me that this is because of the genetic variation between plants. So it's not just a matter of changing the acidity of the soil after all.

< We grow five different photinias; these are very sought after, especially for landscaping.

Lace-cap hydrangeas exude Japanese delicacy.

A Little Touch of Europe

The approach of autumn heralds our busiest period in the nursery. Not only for our 100,000 camellias but also for our famous Paradise polyanthus. This bright, cheery plant reminds me of spring in southern Europe, where it appears outdoors as soon as the weather warms up. In tin wash basins on metal stands, in window boxes, in cane baskets resting on stone fences, in planter boxes outside restaurants; these flowers seem to be the decoration of choice just about everywhere. Each year we grow at least 150,000 polyanthus in the nursery. Of these the very best 10,000 are selected as breeding stock and placed in a separate shadehouse of their own. In August, during our open weekend, visitors swarm down to this house to check out what's new.

"This year," says Carolyn, who is our hybridist, "we are trying to get a few extra petals in fluorescent purple with pointy tips." Or she announces: "See this inner bank of white around the purple bit? We want to change that to yellow and make it wider." The more you look at the individual flowers, the more variety there is to be seen in each and every bloom, even on the same plant. Just the other night, Bob said to me after dinner, "In all the old books about polyanthus there were no true blues at all – they were a sort of motley purple." Well, how far polyanthus breeding has advanced! Now we have over 400 different breeding strains, including some completely new colours. Ruffled double ones, some that look like faded denim jeans, and our superb "frangipani" range, which look just like miniature bicoloured frangipani flowers. Most sensational of all, for me, is the miniature rose collection; these have the prettiest rosebud-shaped flowers. A lovely gift to give on a dull winter's day, and much longer-lasting than any bunch of roses!

We usually plant out thousands of polyanthus in the garden in late

< Bold purple polyanthus look superb when planted out with blue polyanthus.

This delicate pale-blue shade in our polyanthus range is a relatively recent release.

The intricacy of each polyanthus flower never fails to amaze me.

One of our best new polyanthus. Each flower has such a bright, happy face.

An order of polyanthus picked out and ready to go in the nursery.

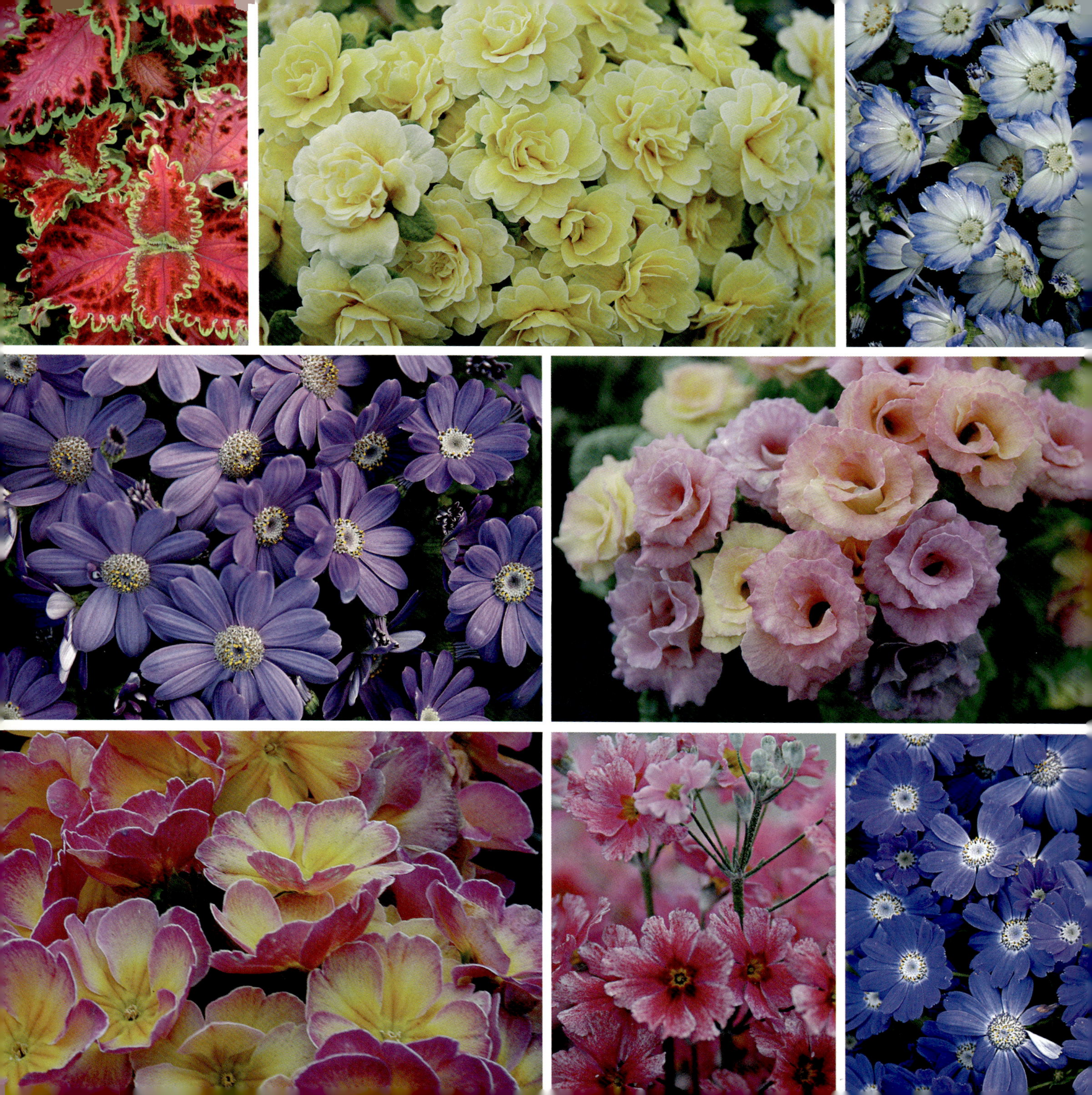

July, in time for our spring open weekend, which is always held on the first weekend in August. Our autumn open weekend is always held on the first weekend in May. During the rest of the year, the garden is open for private tours. The dogs and I really enjoy these visits. Trudy waits with anticipation at the bottom of the stairs for the visitors to alight from the big buses and the exclamations of delight," Oh, there's a little dog here to greet us!" She wags her tail and naturally gets a pat from everyone, and when they finally depart, Trudy is there again at my side, waving everyone goodbye.

< CENTRE L–R Bob breeds a range of cineraria each year in the most extraordinary colours; Our new miniature rose-shaped polyanthus flower in the prettiest shades; Begonias, such as this *Begonia rex*, are another of Bob's favourites that he continues to breed in the nursery.

< BOTTOM L–R In our polyanthus breeding programme, we choose our colour combinations carefully; Bob's *Primula* varieties now rank among the best available; The flowers on this cineraria look like small blue buttons with a white centre.

< TOP L–R Coleus are a favourite with Bob and he has bred many different varieties; Our delicate, ruffled double polyanthus range is delightful; Bi-coloured cineraria look most effective, especially this blue and white variation.

∨ 'Matilda' poppies, which Bob bred fifteen years ago, have become most sought after for their colour range, enormous size and long flowering habit.

Jessee as a puppy, smelling the lavender.

Lavender Pinks

After the polyanthus come the lavenders. Bob has been breeding lavender for the past fifteen years and his efforts have paid off; we now sell one million plants worldwide each year. It is only fairly recently that pink lavender has become available. In 1991 botanists from Kew Gardens and the University of Reading in England discovered a new cerise-red *L. stoechas* species along the coast in south-eastern Spain. From that strain, all the pinks have been developed. Our lavenders now come in all possible shades of pink, as well as the most amazing combinations: pink with white wings, pink with purple wings, purple with red wings, red with white wings…

< A variegated *Eunomyus* border set off this bed of pink lavender superbly last spring.

< Our trial bed of lavenders looks ever so pretty and Provençale.

Our nursery staff enjoy the company of our two dogs. Jessee is the ringleader in the morning as Bob sets off. One bark means "Find your hat", two barks mean "Shoes on", and three barks mean "We're off Dad!" When they arrive at the nursery, just around the time that the staff are arriving too, its pats and hugs and lots of enthusiastic tail-wagging all round. Later in the day I often find the dogs working in the nursery. Especially Trudy, our resident champion ratter. She frequently succeeds in catching bush rats, who make nests between the pots, while Jessee acts as her assistant. Trudy's hunting instinct is in her genes – Cairn Terriers have been catching vermin amongst the lairds' and crofters' piles of rocks, called cairns, in the fields of Scotland for several centuries.

Every week of the year, there is something new and exciting to see in Bob's plant-breeding houses in the nursery. He obtains a great deal of pleasure by slowly driving around suburban streets and seeing his babies flourishing and being enjoyed by others in their gardens. Such is the life of a plant breeder. And I, along with thousands of other people throughout the world, reap the benefit of what he sows.

A Plant Breeder's Delight

∧ Lavender flowers are growing bigger and bigger. Bob's aim is to have them bloom all the way down the stem so that they can be used as an attractive cut flower.

∧ Trudy, our best watchdog, keeping guard by the back door next to pots of lavender.

∧ This cerise-coloured lavender makes a brilliant display wherever it is planted.

∧ Could we ever have imagined lavenders like this twenty years ago?

This lustrous antique vase contrasts well with old-fashioned shades of sweet pea.

Sensational Scents

Our Sweet Pea Patch

The fragrance of a sweet pea is difficult to describe. Unmistakably sweet, yes, but it is a unique and instantly recognisable fragrance. One that has been widely enjoyed for several centuries, ever since the first sweet pea was brought into cultivation around 1700 from Malta and Sicily.

The annual planting of sweet peas is my job. Well, popping the seeds in the ground is. All 1428 of them! Preparing the soil is Bob's job. In his grandiose style, he has constructed our sweet pea trellises on a royal scale. Standing three metres high and averaging about eight metres long, three rows of varying length are enclosed in plastic netting to keep out the bower birds. That's the top sweet pea patch. We have another patch below the chook house, constructed in the same manner.

Bob spreads chicken manure about ten days before planting and then rotary hoes it into the ground. The timing of planting is crucial – preferably St Patrick's Day, 17 March, or a few days thereafter. Last year we travelled overseas in February and I planted the seeds out before we left. Possibly because of that, they failed spectacularly, for the first time in the nine years that I have been planting them. We still do not know exactly what went wrong, but they were certainly not happy. By mid-March the cooler weather has arrived and the humidity has almost gone.

Before the planting day, Bob has raked the area over lightly to remove any little weeds. "Plant them 6 cm from the wire," he instructs me. Unless it rains, I then water each side of the raised beds with a hose daily

< Our splendid top sweet pea patch.

until they germinate – about ten days later. Once the little green shoots are long enough, I attach them to the wires with plastic clips and repeat this several times throughout their growth to train them up as high as possible. Regular watering is essential, as is regular dead-heading to encourage more blooms. August is sweet pea show time for us, but the first flowers usually come out in early June.

We buy our sweet pea seed from Gawler Sweet Peas, north of Adelaide. For many years their flowers have won first prize in the Royal Adelaide Show; I'm convinced they are the best available in Australia. They have gorgeous colours with lots of petals, some are frilly, some spotty or striped, and the fragrance is intense. Best of all, they are winter-flowering, and the only strain that flowers well in the Sydney climate.

Choosing colour combinations is always good fun. We plant pansies in the long bed adjacent to the path outside the top sweet pea patch for a winter and spring display. And often we plant pink *Primula* or blue larkspur immediately in front of the trellis rows. Last year Bob used five rows of yellow pansies as a border. So for the sweet peas I chose blues and lavenders for contrast at one end, shading through to pinks at the other end in the first row. Then I selected lavender to pastel pinks and creams for the second row, with blues to lavender and purples in the last row. The bottom beds ended up with mixed pinks, reds and whites, and just a hint of coral and cream. In between these beds, daffodils and jonquils add the finishing touch. After years of trial and error I finally have the colour scheme I like, so now I simply order the same quantity each year and plant them out. The plastic labels from the previous year, tied on to the wires, are still legible and the whole job is made much easier.

> These frilly sweet peas would always win first prize!

∧ Pink sweet peas are the very essence of romance.

> This double purple stock strain from Tasmania blooms profusely in Paradise.

Sweet Peas Forever

Sweet peas have such a dainty, delicate flower, like silk. On our first visit to Paris together, Bob bought me a large bunch of sweet peas. The florist selected the colours – burgundy with pale pink. Not a combination we would have chosen but, in typical French fashion, they worked a treat and made our hotel room smell so romantic. Whenever we travel, if we are in a place for several nights, Bob and I buy flowers for our room. In Rome especially, we have enjoyed some magnificent blooms, which Bob always arranges. And of course we make sure there are some fragrant flowers among the bunches. Sweet peas look best in a wide-topped vase, so that the blooms can spread out. As they last quite a few days, they are excellent value as a cut flower.

So many people have visited our garden in August over the years and been amazed to see our sweet peas in full bloom. "Why are they flowering now?" is the most common question. "Most of the commercially available ones flower in summer," Bob responds, "but because we have such a hot summer here they only last a short while. These seeds are another line, which has been bred in Australia from a winter-flowering sport."

Stock Supremo

Another nostalgic scent for me is the sweet, intoxicating perfume of stock. It is the same for Bob. Many a time we have driven around old country towns and he has spotted some old-fashioned stock growing in private gardens. We had great success when we visited Tasmania. Double purple stock bloomed amongst anemones and ranunculus in one front garden. When we approached the owner he was only too delighted to offer us seed. The strain, he said, was over forty years old and had been grown by his mother. Another time, Bob, with his eagle eyes for plants, discovered a wonderful double

< You can almost smell the perfume from this magnificent double-pink stock.

pink variety growing down the side of a stone cottage in a small village. The elderly gentleman, who I approached in the backyard, was thrilled that his magnificent stock were being admired and he let us pick the ripening seed. Now both these pink and purple varieties grow in our garden.

Luculia and Lilacs

Soon after Bob and I met, he arrived on my doorstep armed with buckets of flowers to woo me. It was the right way to win my heart. Even as a tiny child, about three years old, I would always pick any flower hanging over a fence when I was out walking. Just one, mind you, but what pleasure it gave me to carry that flower home and place it in water. It seems that Bob was exactly the same. Two obsessed flower lovers from early childhood.

Among the buckets of flowers that Bob brought me that first May were sprays of a shrub which had pretty, glossy leaves around massed heads of small soft-pink flowers. This alluring flower, entirely new to me, had an exquisite perfume, and it was unlike anything else I had ever come across. It was *Luculia*. We now have a grove of around fifty bushes of it, in a sheltered position amongst other plants near the bottom of our garden. It first blooms around the end of April, but has a long flowering season that continues right though until August. We grow not only the single pale pink *Luculia sudetica*, and a single and double white *Luculia intermedia*, but also many hybrids between the two colours in all shades of pink, including a lovely deeper mid-pink.

< Our lovely *Luculia sudetica*.

During my teenage years, I spent my weekends walking for miles in the Adelaide Hills. I was always accompanied by my mother's faithful dog, Trudy, a Cairn Terrier. (Much later, I was to name my own Cairn after her.) Right next to our farm, on a small plot of land, was the Kenton Valley Baptist church, built in 1849. And in that old churchyard grew lilac bushes with double flowers in shades of purple and lavender. How many times I entered those grounds just to inhale the perfume – and, of course, to pick a few branches to take home, since the church was no longer in use. Even now I can recall the lyrics of "California Dreamin'", the song by The Mamas and The Papas; it used to play so often at that time, on the little radio I always carried with me:

∧ Pink double stock, from seed given to Bob in Tasmania, growing in a raised bed with blue violas.

" Bob ... arrived on my doorstep armed with buckets of flowers to woo me "

> Lovely lilac blooms are subtle and yet so sensationally scented.

Stopped into a church
I passed along the way
Well I got down on my knees
And I pretend to pray

The love of lilac still lingers in my life. I have recently purchased several plants, which I have been assured will flourish in our semi-tropical conditions. I await the results but, for the record, the plants growing are: *Syringa persica*, with a soft mauve flower, *S. vulgaris* 'Charles Joly' with purplish-red double flowers, *S. vulgaris* 'Marceau' (from France) with soft lilac-coloured double flowers, *S. afghanica* with a small mauve-purple double flower, and the dark pink *S. josikaea* (from Hungary). I know lilacs can grow in our area because Dorothy Hitchcock, from the Kulnura Garden Club, once showed me a very old bush of double purple lilac growing near her house. Unfortunately the piece we took did not strike, but it was living proof that some lilacs can indeed grow very well in our climate. Time will tell with my new purchases.

" the love of lilac still lingers in my life "

Fragrances of Tahiti

The fragrance of gardenias reminds me of Tahiti. A tropical paradise where one can revel in the enhanced perfumes, which are always so much stronger in warm places. Not surprisingly, given their heady fragrance, gardenias are closely related to *Luculia*. In fact they belong to the same family, Rubicea. The fragrance from several bushes of *Gardenia grandiflora* wafts into our bedroom on a summer evening – pure bliss. Although they barely last a couple of days as a cut flower, I cannot resist picking small bunches to place strategically throughout the house. Their waxy, creamy white double flowers are so perfect, and even the single starry groundcover version, *Gardenia* 'Superstar' appeals to me because of its sensational scent.

I once asked the late and great gardening writer and photographer, Stirling Macoboy, what his favourite flower was. To my surprise he answered, without hesitation, "the frangipani". When I asked why, he explained that it was because of their beauty and variety. In fact, over 400 different frangipani are in cultivation. I had no idea, having only seen the creamy yellow flowers and the occasional apricot or dark red ones when visiting Brisbane on business trips over the years. The word frangipani sounds Italian, as indeed it is. It was an Italian scent, manufactured in the 16th century, that was named after Marquis Frangipani. It became famous as the perfume used to scent the boxes in which gloves were stored. When the flower was discovered, it was named after this perfume because the fragrance was so similar.

∧ The colour and fragrance of *Gardenia grandiflora* perfect this arrangement that Bob made for our Christmas table.

< The perfume of *Osmanthus delavayi* 'Heaven Scent' fills the air.

Last year I planted a very special glowing pink frangipani that grows in Hawaii. I sent away to "The Frangipani Gardens" in Queensland for it and they very obligingly cut a piece from their own tree for me. It's called 'Cool Aid', and so far it has made slow progress. Another that I am about to order is evocatively named 'Polynesian Sunset'. It is a brilliant pink, touched with orange. Bob thinks my efforts are a waste of time as they won't grow here. Once again, time will tell.

Osmanthus and Heliotrope

It is hard to believe that the sweet-smelling *Osmanthus* is part of the olive family. *Osmanthus delavayi* 'Pearly Gates' and 'Heaven Scent' are planted throughout our garden. This is yet another shrub that I did not know about before I met Bob. And in China, osmanthus-flavoured biscuits are among the nicest I have tasted.

Heliotropium arborescens, or heliotrope, commonly called "cherry pie", on the other hand, I have enjoyed for many years. It smells just like vanilla, and flowers for most of the year in our climate. It is such an old-fashioned, pretty addition to the garden and makes a lovely border along the edge of many of our pathways.

∧ *Heliotropium arborescens* perfumes the garden near our house.

> Frangipani, otherwise known as *Plumeria acutifolia*.

Buddleia

Often known as the "butterfly bush", it is the sweet smell of honey that attracts butterflies to *Buddleia* shrubs. My very favourite is the large pink-flowered *Buddleia davidii* 'Pink Delight'. *Buddleia* is more commonly grown in purple or lilac shades, but there are also white and red varieties. One hybrid that Bob has bred is called 'Wattle Bird'. It grows extraordinarily fast and its yellow flowers make a wonderful display in the garden. Another useful white variety released by Bob is *Buddleia asiatica* 'Spring Promise'; its scent is reminiscent of freesias. It is interesting that some plants have the ability to mimic the perfume of others. On one trip to China we discovered a daphne that was not a daphne – it was just mimicking its perfume and appearance. Likewise we found a lilac that was not a lilac, yet identical in fragrance and flower format. Quite incredible, but apparently it's all to do with attracting insects for pollination. Or, in other words, the instinct for survival.

∧ The yellow of Bob's *Buddleia* hybrid 'Wattle Bird' is enhanced by plantings of blue and white pansies.

< The beautiful form of the blooms of this white *Buddleia davidii* would lighten up any garden.

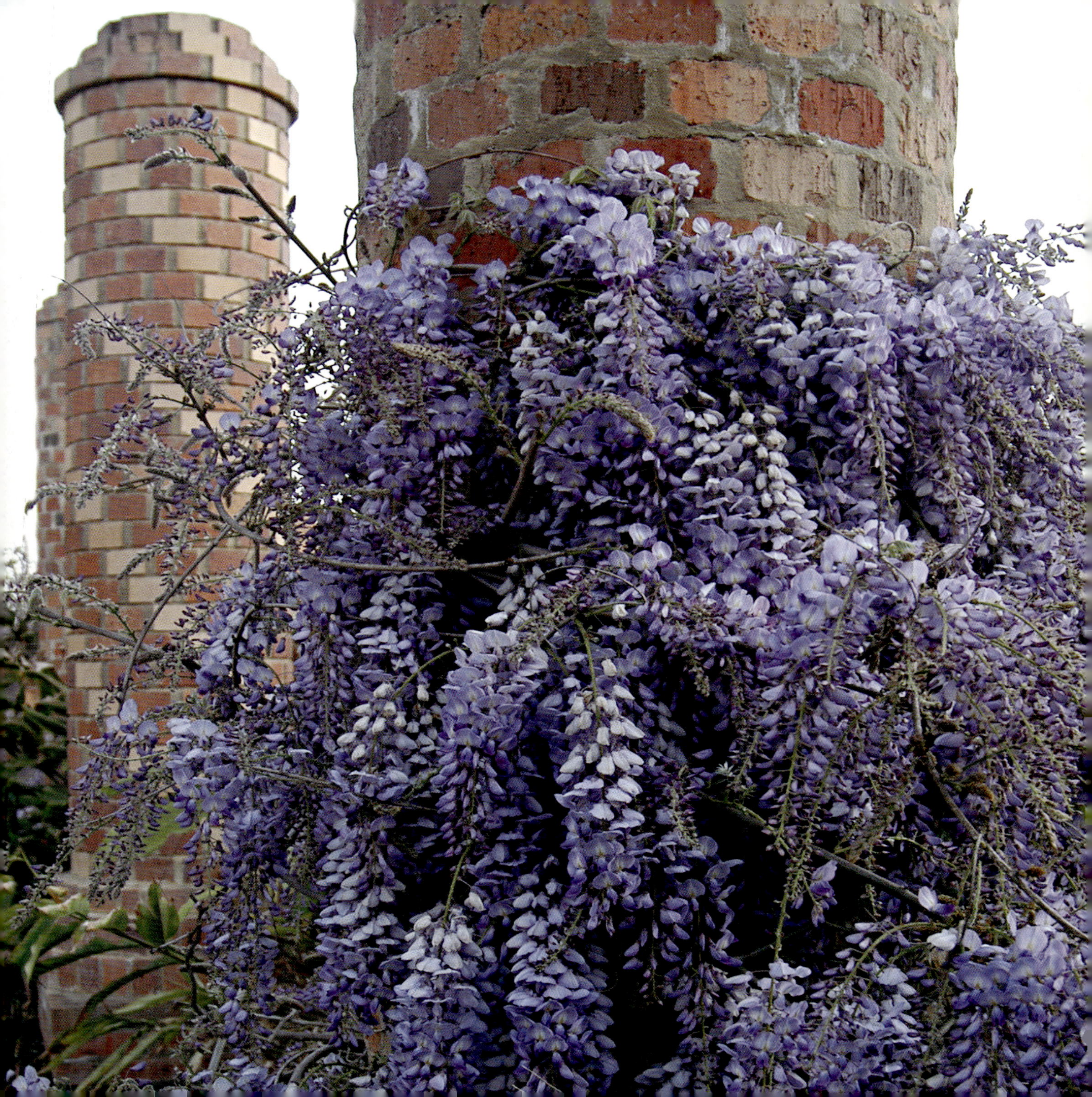

When the Wisteria Blooms

For three weeks from late September through to October, the garden is enveloped in another heady perfume that intoxicates me. The *Wisteria* is out! When I drive home and park in the carport beneath its shade and fragrance, I enter a different world. One that is sensuous and sensational. Our long *Wisteria* walk is all planted with the same variety – the common mauve *Wisteria sinensis*, which Bob considers to be the best of all. This species has been grown in Chinese gardens for several thousand years. Our pergola now extends about 50 metres, and Bob is making another one, of equal length, below the chook house.

Climbing up our belvedere, near the summer house, is the most delicate lavender pink *Wisteria floribunda* 'Honbeni', which I cannot wait to sit under when it is in flower. And, right down at the bottom of the garden, Bob has planted twenty-six of the very best different varieties of *Wisteria* to form a shady walkway.

∧ Sweet William comes in a variety of gorgeous shades, all with such a pleasing fragrance.

Divine Dianthus

The word *Dianthus* derives from the Greek language. It translates as "divine healing flower dedicated to Zeus" (one of the Greek gods). This small, dainty, long-flowering plant has an intense fragrance of cloves and is one of the constant delights in our garden. The genus includes carnations, "pinks" and sweet william, and it is believed that the early Romans used them to flavour wine. By the 15th century they were growing in Eastern Europe and England, and by the end of the 17th century 400 *Dianthus* cultivars were listed in catalogues. Shakespeare

< A simple brick pillar looks ever so pretty with a skirt of *Wisteria* wrapped around it.

referred to them in his plays, and Henry VIII loved them too.

With names like 'Laced Monarch', 'Devon Magic' and 'Widecombe Fair', they conjure up images of English country gardens. The variety 'Mrs Simkins White', which is over 100 years old, thrives in our garden and has such a lacy, old-world appearance. And the differences between the varieties are remarkable. Some have a red velvet texture highlighted with rose pink, others are a soft pale peach, another is bright pink, and yet another, called 'Doris', has very pretty pink and peach tonings – all with the most glorious fragrance. Some have a fine picotee edging, and others are striped or streaked, or just one colour. Perfect in the garden and as a cut flower too, they enhance and perfume any space indoors or outdoors.

< This arrangement of mixed *Dianthus* is one of my special favourites for perfume and prettiness.

Dianthus 'Joy' makes a splendid border for one of our rose beds.

Our troll guards the entrance to Bob's Roman bridge.

The Follies of Bob

"Bob is a reincarnation of a Roman stonemason."

The Bridge that Bob Built

Sometimes I think Bob is a reincarnation of a Roman stonemason. How else to explain his uncanny ability to transform stone into all sorts of magical structures – walls, paths, columns, pillars, a bandstand and even a bridge. The bridge that he built looks like the small 2000-year-old Roman bridges that are still used in Wales. Our solid stone bridge, with one single arch, spans a small gully

∨ Bob's Roman bridge.

\> Jessee, with Trudy not far behind, crossing our bridge.

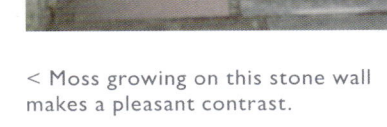

< Moss growing on this stone wall makes a pleasant contrast.

that Bob excavated many years ago. All garden visitors walk over it to reach our Summer House, where tables and chairs are set out under cover for their morning tea or lunch.

Ever since he has lived in Paradise, Bob has collected stone on the property during his walks. Heaps of ironstone and sandstone are now scattered everywhere waiting to be used. "See this piece here," he points out to an interested spectator, "you could use it side on, but it would look more unusual and effective if this end bit was sticking out." Even though they look like dry-stone walls, Bob actually uses cement to hold his walls together – but in such a way that it is hidden from the front. His imaginative flair with stone and bricks is

\> Decorative brickwork, seen through our "Stairway to Heaven".

legendary. Most amazing of all, however, he is self-taught. It just all comes naturally to him. On last count, Bob announced, "We have used over 450,000 bricks around the place." Bricks, which form many of the paths between our garden beds, also feature in retaining walls and ornamental columns with stunning results.

Ancient Athens in Paradise?

"What's going on over there – is it a recreation of ancient Athens?" visitors commonly ask when they discover our fifty "Greek columns" for the first time. The plan is to extend the *Wisteria* walk right along these columns with a steel treillage (trellis) across the top to support

> The "crazy wall" under construction, using all sorts of rubble.

∨ Jessee supervises Bob as he works on his new stone steps.

∧ "Watch this space," Bob tells me, "I'm building a 1.7 metre high Trudy here." A few days later I realise he is making a stone cairn, not a cairn dog!

the wisteria. About halfway along this line of columns is an arched brick entrance which I call our "stairway to heaven". "But," points out Bob, "you go down through it, not up". "This is Bob's crazy wall" I tell garden groups when we arrive at the bottom of the garden. To which they respond, "Ah, yes, I can see that!"

Our quirky gargoyles, lurking around many corners, are either much loved or hated. Trudy's face is one of the characters peering from the gargoyle wall fountain and I always point out her image to visitors. And then I turn the tap on to release trickles of water, which spout from the eyes, ears, mouth or nostrils of twelve very weird faces. The rectangular area in front of this fountain is to be laid with mosaics, just like in a Roman courtyard. "Where are the monkeys?" inquire so

< The columns on the oriental-style wall near our tea plantation all have individual stone crowns.

> Not yet completed, our bandstand (on the left) overlooks a series of ponds used for recycling water.

Our row of "ancient" Greek columns.

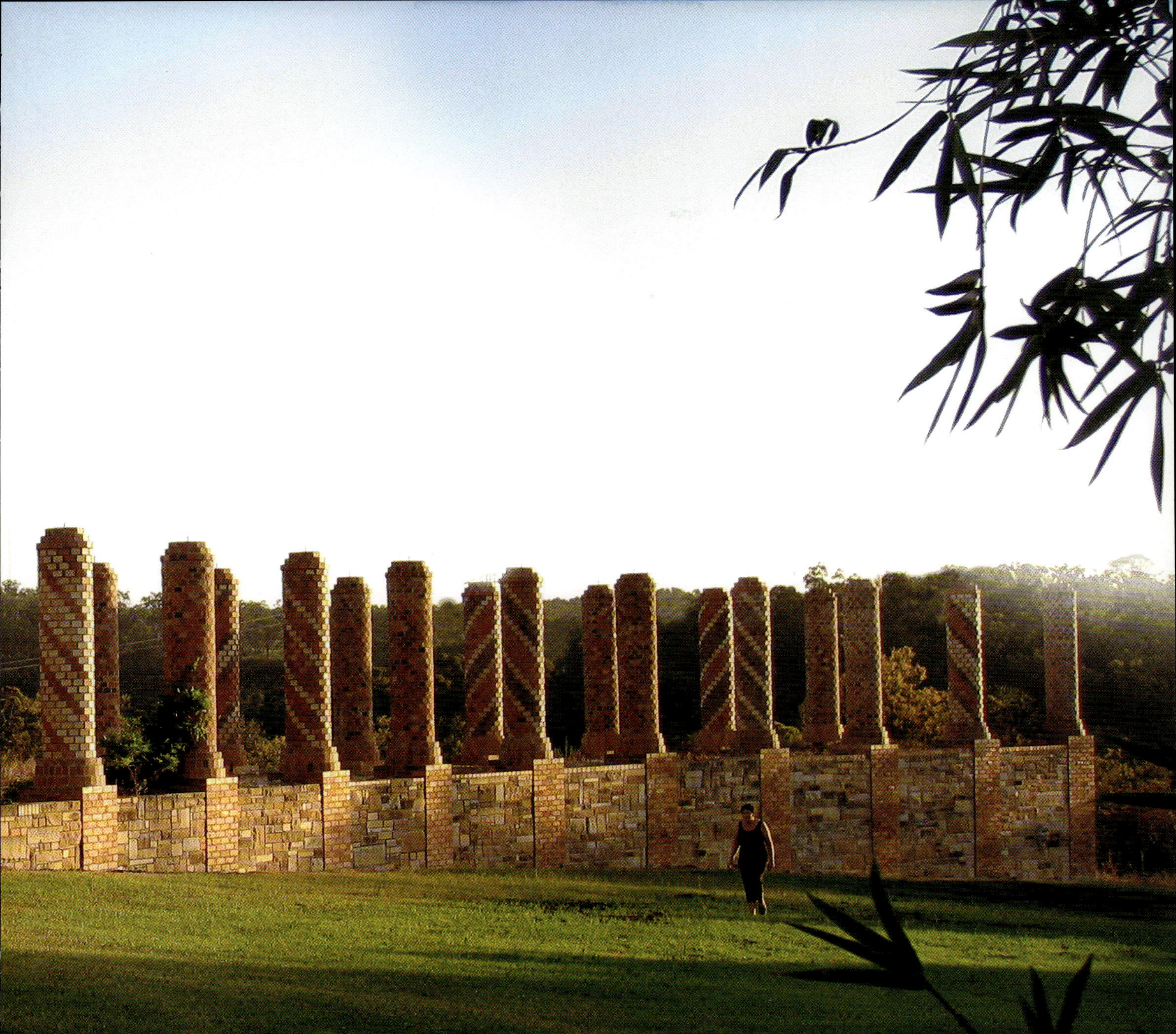

∧ *Incarvillea arguta*, grown from seed that Bob collected in Szechuan, China, spills over the edge of the "crazy wall".

> Instead of gargoyles, I would prefer angels, such as this Italian one to appear in our garden.

many visitors. Our "monkey colony" has become quite famous and adds another dimension to the garden. Full of cheeky characters, the monkeys were sculpted by Leon Loreaux. Bob often points out past Prime Ministers amongst the group and children love to have their photographs taken standing or sitting next to them.

Bob's decorative work around the garden is not restricted to brick

" There is no overall plan, it just evolves "

> The dogs often take themselves for walks along our many pathways.

and stones. Numerous steel structures, which have been galvanized to prevent rust, are used in a variety of different ways. The clever Tony Tabone, or our energetic and multitalented Maintenance Manager Ross Darby, make these creations from Bob's instructions – he draws the designs out, by foot, on the ground. Sometimes, but not always, a paper plan eventuates.

We even have our own "Eiffel Tower", with a lattice bower underneath it in which to rest and enjoy the surroundings. I gave it this name because it has a definite French style, as does our superb belvedere. Bob has read many books on architectural designs from around the world; and on our travels, if there is some feature he particularly likes, we take a photograph. He stores much of this information in his fertile mind and can retrieve it when necessary. One tower that he created in the garden I call "Rapunzel's Tower". It is a wonderful stone tower, topped with jagged pieces of stone sticking right up into the air. I know exactly where Bob's inspiration for this came from as one day I was looking through some of his old slides and came across a picture of virtually the same tower. "It was in an Irish garden that I once visited," he explained when I asked him about it. I am wondering what our visit to Barcelona this year will bring forth in his mind, after he sees Antoni Gaudi's famous cathedral there.

> Two lions, imported from France, greet visitors as they enter Paradise. Our observatory is in the background.

< Bob made this stone "wall flower" just for me.

> The figures in this "Teddy Bears' Picnic" were made by Joy Stephens, who was our trusty gardener for many years. Her husband, Noel, was Bob's wonderful Maintenance Manager for over twelve years.

" When I was six years old, I used to spend hours building clay dams in roadside drains: when they were full of water I would blow them up with crackers. " BOB CHERRY

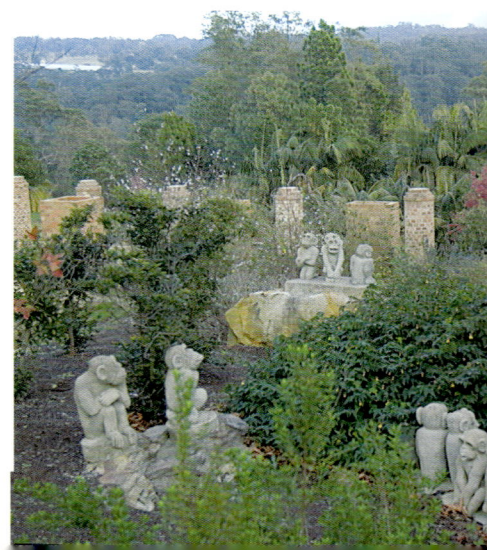

> Construction of our spectacular valley which will include four ponds linked by cascades of water. And three ornate steel bridges from which to look down upon hundreds of lotus.

< The biggest monkey is Bob, the boss monkey.

Bob also works with wood and copper. Our observatory is constructed of wood, as is a house for shade-loving plants. The brick church window, amidst the cherry trees on the top driveway, has a roof made of shingles; and beneath it, Bob has carved out a grotto. He is looking for a statue of Saint Fiacre (the patron saint of gardeners) to place there, but has not yet found one that appeals.

Our obelisk, 8 metres high, stands proudly at the bottom of the garden. Bob is unsure if he made it high enough, but he can always change it later. Everything is in a state of evolution, and he has always constructed the garden accordingly, although his beds must be wide enough for a succession of graded plants – taller shrubs and trees at the back, taller annuals and then lower annuals right at the front. But it's all a matter of constant revision. His motto is "if something doesn't work, change it".

It's the same with his landscaping of the property. "I don't know what I'm doing 'til I do it," he claims. "But you must have a master plan," retort so many visitors. Yet, there is no overall plan – it just evolves, literally according to the lie of the land; how steep it is, how rocky it is, and what would work best. One of the problems here is that we have shallow soil in some places, so to encourage more growth, Bob has deliberately built walls to add depth to the beds where trees will be planted. One of the first major jobs he undertook in Paradise was to build a dam in front of the house. It was to be an important component of the nursery, for recycling water. Later, he extended it to make a huge lake and added a canyon at one end.

< The monkeys are one of the star attractions in Paradise.

A Constant State of Flux

Our barbecue house features intriguing dragons on its copper roof.

The gargoyle wall fountain looks even better when the maples are colouring in autumn.

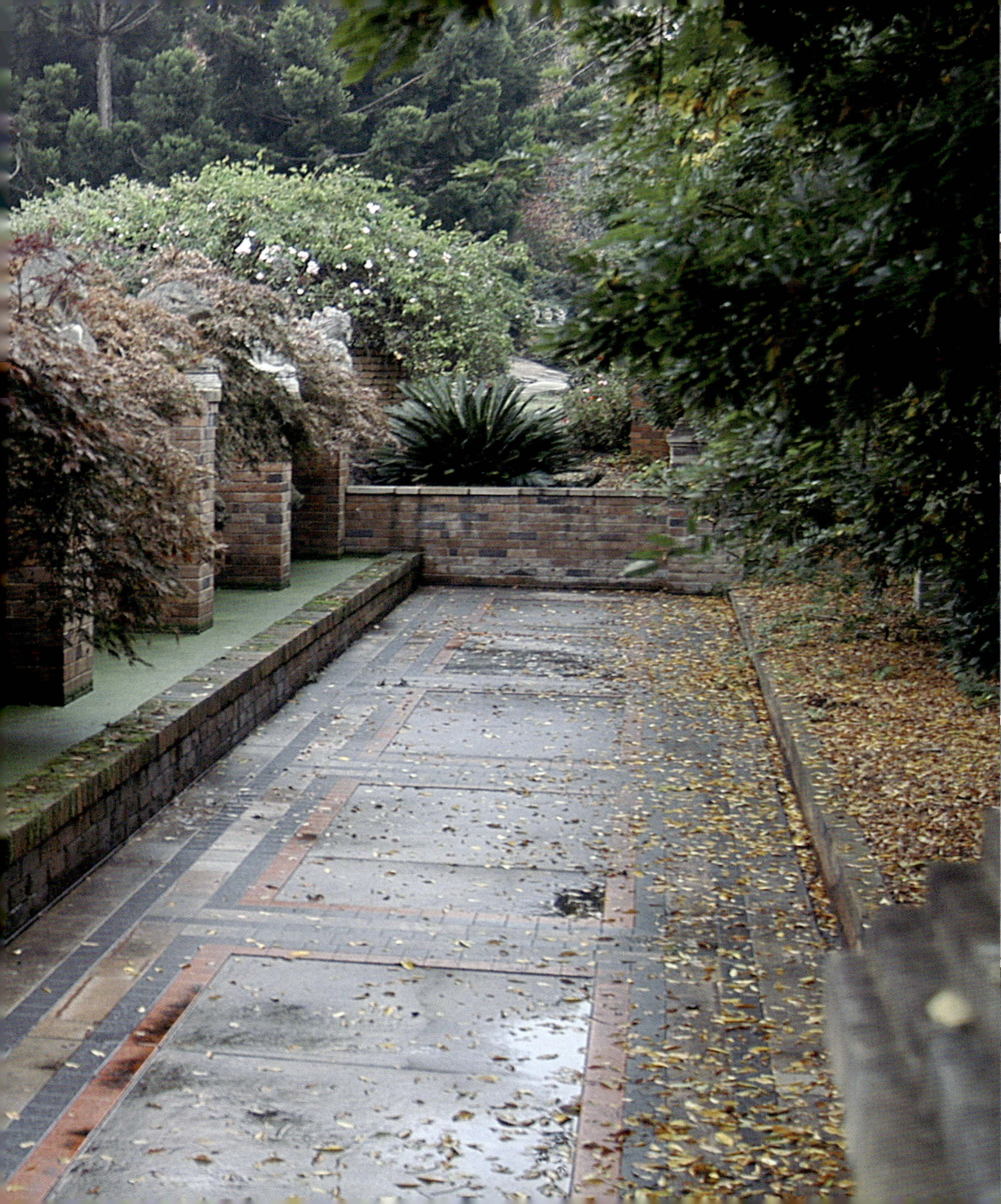

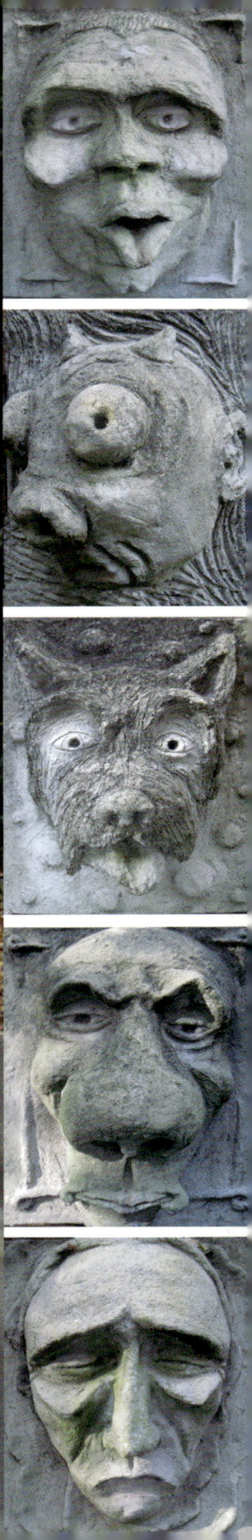

∧ Our obelisk towers over
the bottom of the garden.

< Kookaburras regularly
alight on our "Eiffel Tower".

Thinking about the way in which Bob comes up with his ideas, I conclude that he was born in the wrong age. About 300 years too late. I can visualise him striding around an English estate, overseeing scores of minions as they implement his latest design. What fun he would have had working on such a grand scale, and what a magnificent garden he would have created. Not many people have the ability to visualise, in their mind's eye, the end result. But Bob always gets it right. And if by chance he's not happy with the result, he can always change it.

∧ Pink *Wisteria*, when in flower on our enchanting belvedere, will inspire all who stand under it.

> An arched entrance leads into the King's Garden.

This Cardiocrinum giganteum var. yunnanense in China was taller than me!

Botanising with Bob

Sticks and Stones

Both Bob and I are obsessed with travelling as well as flowers. In our early days together I loved hearing about his adventures searching for plants in exotic parts of the world. Our first expedition together, only eight months after we met, was to Vietnam in December 1999. I remember celebrating my birthday with a dinner in the hotel where we were staying, somewhere between Sapa and Hanoi. Scattered around the garden, for the entertainment of patrons, were a variety of animals – including a tiger, brown bears, and some gigantic, very nasty looking Burmese pythons. The only trouble was, they were alive and their cages looked very shaky!

Since those early days we have travelled extensively, always on the lookout for new plant varieties in places as far flung (from Australia) as the Azores, Iran and Armenia. But it is not only plants that attract our interest. Everything can inspire us, from the texture of walls and the shapes of all the different bridges we come across, to the colour scheme of annuals in a village square. Bob's imagination goes into overdrive as he stores up everything he likes for future use. And I record our likes, and sometimes our dislikes, in photographs.

∧ This fantastic underground cistern in Istanbul dates back to 532 AD. It's a wonder Bob hasn't yet created a similar one in Paradise!

< It was the ambience and colour of the walls that drew my attention to this courtyard in Venice. I later discovered that the house had belonged to the famous Italian playwright Carlo Goldoni, who lived there in the 18th century.

> The intricate stonework at the Alhambra in Granada, Spain, is unequalled anywhere in the world.

A Dream Come True

< Before I met Bob, I had never seen bluebells growing wild in England.

∧ A total of 409 bridges span the 117 tiny islands that make up Venice.

It was a misty morning in Guilin, China, when Bob and I discovered a series of superb moon bridges.

In my twenties, I read biographies and autobiographies – as many as I could get my hands on. Bob at that age was passionately reading everything he could about plant collecting. He spent his evenings devouring every book that was then available on the subject. He was especially interested in the old English collectors, like George Forrest and Kingdom Ward, who collected in China where the richest flora in the world was to be found.

In his mind's eye, Bob saw drifts of rhododendrons, valleys of *Magnolia campbellii*, cherry walks and birch groves, all spread out in his lovely future garden. Although he could not grow the plants that they described at high altitudes, their exploits still thrilled him. Occasionally these intrepid collectors would visit the warmer, lower altitude forests in Burma and China. They talked about discovering trees such as *Gordonia*, *Schima*, forests of *Camellia*, jasmine, *Primula* and many other treasures, and recorded: "We considered these plants would not be hardy in the U.K., so we did not collect them." Bob says he used to cry out in dismay and mutter, "You could have sent them to Australia!"

Bob eventually visited China himself in 1984. It had just been opened up to the

81

This waterwheel, used to irrigate the surrounding fields in Vietnam, was one of the finest we have ever seen.

West, and he went with a group of *Camellia* enthusiasts from the International Camellia Society. But much to his disappointment, he was not allowed to roam the hills or collect plants. However, Bob's fame as a *Camellia* breeder was spreading, and five years later a group of botanists from the Kunming Botanic Gardens visited Paradise. They suggested that Bob join a six-week collecting trip in eastern China that the Sydney Royal Botanic Gardens was planning for the following year. But just a few weeks prior to departure, the Tiananmen Square massacre occurred and the New South Wales Government put a halt to the planned botanical trip.

Notwithstanding, Bob's Chinese friends rang him and said that he was still welcome to come, and that he could bring five friends. Best of all, he would be allowed to collect plants and seeds! Over five weeks, the small group covered 5000 miles of poor roads throughout much of Yunnan, from the high altitudes down to the hot and steamy valleys, collecting over 400 different plants. Since then Bob has visited China more than forty times, always travelling with companions who have mutual interests. And yet, after all these visits, he still only speaks two words of Chinese!

< Bob collected seed from this Engelhardtia spicata *on our first botanising trip together to North Vietnam. It was growing at 2000 m above sea level, and now thrives in our garden.*

> FROM TOP The Chinese countryside has enchanting surprises, such as this delightful bamboo pavilion; It is obvious where the inspiration for so many Chinese paintings comes from; Chinese golden-glazed roof tiles are typically made to look like bamboo.

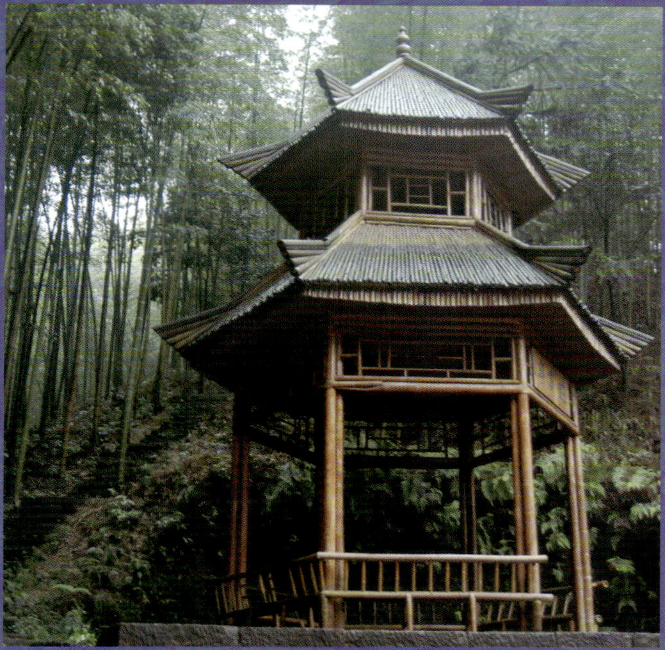
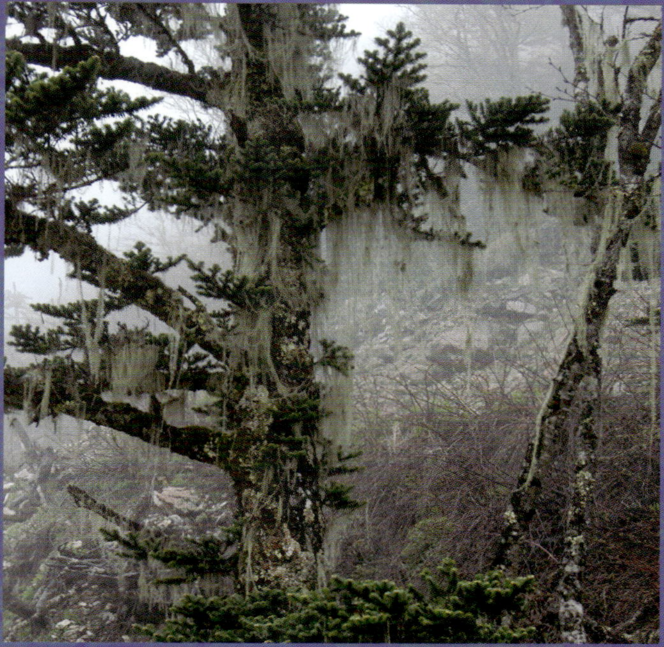
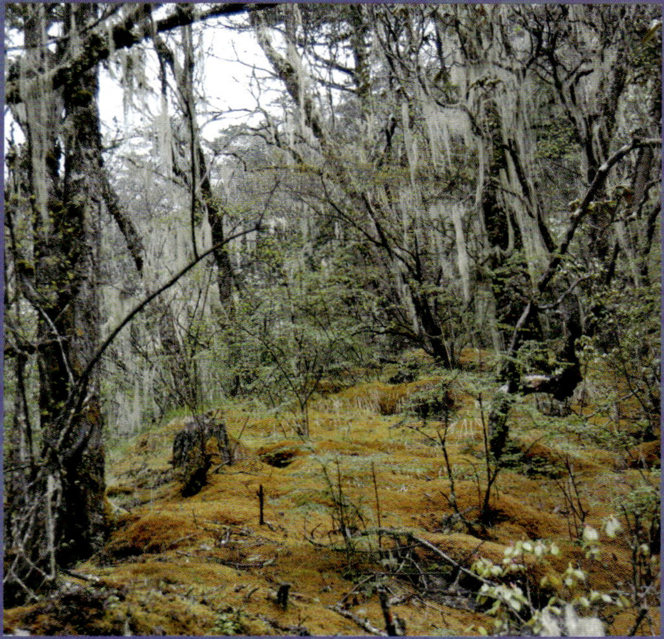
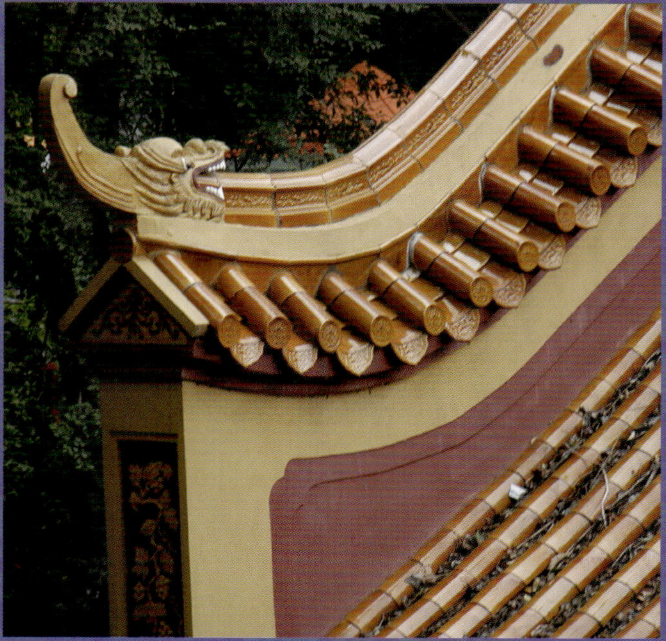

Not Another Mountain!

> Colourful *Cuphea*, bred from seed that Bob collected in Mexico, flower well in our garden.

v Wildflowers of Armenia: *Euphorbia*, forget-me-not, buttercup, cornflower, adonis and *Gladiolus*.

We are standing 2300 metres above sea level in a remote part of China. The road we left behind is 360 metres below us in the valley. Up and up we climb, along treacherous slippery rocks. The mist is swirling around and my legs have turned to jelly. Suddenly I take flight mid-air, but the guide immediately behind grabs me and saves me from toppling down the 50-metre cliff on my left. Feeling sick and light-headed, I pause to rest while Bob streaks ahead like a mountain goat. I try to remember that I am lucky, being the only female participating in this excursion, amongst this group of important botanic researchers. Suddenly, seemingly out of nowhere, we hear *"Camellia!"* I swear Bob can smell where camellias grow! Even after twenty-five years of looking at plants in the wild, he still gets excited when he finds another *Camellia*.

< Bob and I both adore the fields of wild poppies in Spain.

I suppose it's because there's a chance it might be an entirely new species. On this day alone we find five species, including one that nobody in the group has ever heard of, and another with clusters of pink and white flowers. Bob is delighted at such a successful day. When I ask him why he likes collecting plants so much, he replies: "It's nice to see something you know about growing in its natural state."

Our hotel that evening is an incredibly romantic Chinese hideaway, tucked into a cliff in the lower mountains next to a river. Our entertainment after dinner is to be Miao (the local people) dancing. But I am more concerned with other matters: Keep muddy shoes on when going to toilet, as it is located under the shower. Put heat plaster on right shoulder to ease pain caused by constant path surveillance when walking up and down mountains. Sleep in socks worn for last four days and knickers for last two, which look extremely sexy with my long white cotton nightie, to keep out possible bedbugs. All this to find another *Camellia* species! The Chinese reports of our visit in the local newspapers prove it is all worthwhile – they are delighted to have experts visiting their country who can assist in preserving rare camellias that are in danger of extinction.

It requires an experienced and sharp eye to spot something different when wandering among thousands of plants in the wild. When we are looking for lavender in Spain and Portugal, Bob tells me what characteristics to look for and we stride out in opposite directions. I have a good eye, says Bob. I am sure it stems from all the practice I had wandering in the Adelaide Hills after school finished when I was about ten years old. Every afternoon in spring, I would vanish into the bush and wander for hours and miles, collecting enormous bunches of wildflowers. To find a spider orchid was a real

∧ We sometimes stumble across strange beasts, such as this mighty elephant that Bob tried to ride in outback Portugal.

> Looking at lavender, in Spain and Portugal, is one of our favourite pastimes.

85

Bob has promised to make me a studio, so I constantly photograph appealing stone cottages, such as this one in Portugal, to encourage him.

Walking down the same hill in Portugal, I discovered yet another lovely little old cottage.

Bob can immediately identify Roman roads, such as this, where we stopped to have lunch one day in Portugal. I could almost visualise chariots charging along it, filled with warriors.

A group of ponies that attracted my attention and led to my rose discovery on the outskirts of Kanding in China.

triumph as they camouflaged themselves so well. I learnt to recognise where they were likely to grow and would usually find one or two! And there were always plenty of bulldog and puppydog orchids (also called donkey orchids) nearby. Nearly all of that scrubland, behind the Lobethal Primary School, where Dad was headmaster for several years before he retired to our dairy farm, has now been cleared. Anyway, it would be considered far too dangerous today for a child to wander up and down those hills alone. I was the lucky one.

On one occasion I stumbled, quite by accident, over the most gorgeous pink lavender in northern Portugal. And another time Bob spotted a very blue lavender, high up on a bank, as we drove up a windy mountain road. But it was quite impossible to stop anywhere for further investigation! I have learnt that plant hunting is full of exciting surprises, and sometimes disappointments as well. Just like real life. Nevertheless, travelling with an obsessed plant hunter is infectious. It is most definitely a disease!

My very first trip to China was with a small group led by Martyn Rix. It was an opportunity not to be missed. How well I remembered watching his television series with Roger Phillips in the early 1990s, "The Quest for the Rose". I simply could not wait for the next episode.

So naturally I brought along a copy of their rose book, which was written to accompany the BBC series, to help identify the many wild roses that I hoped to see along the way. Towards the end of the trip we were staying in the fascinating town of Kanding, which is in the province of Sichuan, near the Tibetan border. We were there for four nights, and on the third evening our bus passed a group of gaily decorated ponies on the way back to our hotel. The next morning I

^ With my camera in a plastic bag, I was ready for adventure!

My Rose Discovery

" those little horses fascinated me "

> The stunning *Rosa moyesii* that I discovered by chance.

decided to do my own thing while the remainder of the party went off in the bus again. Those little horses fascinated me! As most of the others were avid plant hunters like Bob, I would not really be missed.

So I stayed behind to indulge in my love of wandering around old towns, with the added challenge of possibly spotting a different rose. Conversing in sign language, I took a taxi to the outskirts of town, where I had seen the ponies gathered. Further non-verbal communication ensued and I found myself on the back of one, heading up a hill out of town! Although I had no idea whatsoever where I was going, I decided to literally go along for the ride! An obliging woman, who spoke not a word of English, was gently holding the reins, so expert riding skills, something that I lack, were not required.

We climbed up a rough track, higher and higher, over a stream with a rustic stone bridge and up a narrow valley. I was enjoying myself immensely and was not the least bit nervous. I noticed a striking red rose, growing near the water, and made a mental note to check it out on the way back. That is, assuming we returned by the same route!

The road came to an end up at the top of the mountain where, it turned out, there was a cable car. I remember its empty cars sailing past in solitary splendour with the most melancholy Chinese music blaring out into the surroundings. I felt like I was in some strange movie; it was quite eerie. But I was not perturbed. Using some more sign language I dismounted from my horse, which I am sure felt very relieved that it did not have to cart me back down the mountain.

After thoroughly exploring the whole area, I began my descent down the hill. The red rose I had spotted on the way up had such a striking colour and robust appearance that I plucked a couple

^ This bonsai *Pyracantha* was the finest I have ever seen. The art of bonsai originates from the 3rd century AD in China and derives its name from the Chinese "pun sai", which translates as "tree in a pot".

of flowers for identification and took numerous photos. Later that evening I laid out my rose findings for the day on the bed and waited for the others to return.

Much to my genuine amazement and absolute delight, Martyn was terribly excited about what I had found. He checked my copy of his roses book and decided that I had, in ignorant bliss, rediscovered the brilliant red form of *Rosa moyesii*, which was last collected in the wild by Ernest Wilson in 1903! And, furthermore, it was the rose that the group knew grew in that area and had been searching for during the previous days, but had not managed to find! When we departed from Kanding early the next morning, Martyn poked his camera out the bus window to record the location of the hidden valley for his next trip. And when I recently read, in David Austin's latest book *The English Rose*, that the only true red rose found in the wild is *Rosa moyesii*, I was even more ecstatic. Incredibly, I had managed to rediscover a sub-species!

> The rustic stone bridge en route to my *Rosa moyesii*.

Bob's Gordonia Story

We were travelling along the Burma Road in south-west Yunnan. It was still a dirt road in those days, and it snaked around the mountains and dipped down thousands of metres to cross the mighty Mekong River. Then up again and around the Gaoligong Range, which forms the southern end of the Himalayas.

When we entered the Salween River valley, the surrounding wet forest became a veritable spring fairyland for a gardener. Rhododendrons abounded in hills spotted with pink cherry blossom, *Camellia reticulata*, *Hydrangea* and many thousands of other wondrous plants. When we saw small trees with large white flowers growing in a valley next to the road, we quickly stopped the bus. The roadside verge was covered in fallen blooms and whilst the others in the group rushed off to reach the plants in the valley, I decided to remain where I was and survey the scene before selecting the choicest plant to head to. I leant against a large tree trunk, equal in girth to an enormous *Eucalyptus*, and contemplated where all the fallen blooms around me had come from. Much to my amazement, when I looked up I found that the majestic tree towering above me for at least 40 metres was a *Gordonia*.

We subsequently collected seed and on returning to Australia I grew several hundred plants. Three or four years later they flowered, and the blooms ranged between 10 and 20 cm in diameter, with a colour variation from pure white to cream. The leaf colour, from dark green to glossy dark green, confirmed just how variable this species is. From these varieties, we eventually selected three to name including 'Paradise Moonlight'.

^ The spectacular *Gordonia* flower, sometimes likened to a fried egg!

> Chopsticks, left out to dry in a village in China, made a fascinating sight.

" a veritable spring fairyland for a gardener "

< Chrysanthemums are native to China, where they have been grown for 5000 years. Golden yellow was their original colour in the wild, but there are now some amazing varieties, all of which are on sale in Chinese markets. They are often called "spider" or "fantasy" chrysanthemums, for obvious reasons!

Collecting in the 21st Century

These days, things are very different for plant collectors. In 1993 the FAO International Code of Conduct for Plant Germplasm Collecting and Transfer was introduced. As a result, plants belonging to the country of origin cannot be taken out without permission from the authorities. The Australian Quarantine and Inspection Service also requires you to have a permit, which must be surrendered with the plant material for inspection upon arrival in Australia.

Yet it is because of plant collectors that such diversity is now available for home gardeners through their local nurseries. Without people like Bob continuing the tradition of plant collecting and breeding, gardening would be nowhere near as pleasurable.

< When we had a few hours to fill one morning in Guilin, I decided to get dressed up as a "Chinese Princess". Bob was greatly amused watching the transformation!

> It is wonderful to see new varieties at the regular shows held by the Royal Horticultural Society at Vincent Square in London, and at other venues in Chelsea and Birmingham. Attending flower shows, like the Hampton Court Palace Flower Show, is all part of our botanising.

∧ Even when we eat, we can still botanise. This delightful instant potted garden in Rome, drew us into the osteria behind for dinner one evening.

∧ Bob chose this hat for me in England – but as I'm not really a hat person, we left it in the shop. It was hardly suitable for botanising!

∧ We miss our two dogs so much when we are travelling that we have to cuddle other people's dogs, like this West Highland Terrier in England.

We always visit the Palatine Hill when in Rome. Plum blossom was in flower on our last visit, and I am sure Bob feels quite at home among the ruins, some of which date back to the 10th century BC.

Looking up to our church window is magical when the cherry blossom is out.

Spring Blossom

∧ This *Prunus* species is native to Vietnam.

Cherry Delight

Cherry trees in the Cherrys' garden. Appropriately, Bob has planted many of them. He adores their prettiness – as do I and the thousands of visitors who come to our August open weekend, when spring arrives early in Paradise. Although the cherry blossom season is fleeting and over all too quickly, it is worth waiting for. I inspect the tiny buds for days ahead in eager anticipation. In good weather, with no wind, the blossom can linger for two weeks; but some years, it is over in a few days.

< Cherry blossom petals form a carpet beneath the *Argyranthemum* (Marguerite daisy) bush.

∧ *Magnolia* blooms perfectly complement the lattice timber on our observatory in the background.

∧ *Prunus* 'Louise Audrey', one of Bob's chance hybrids of *P. campanulata* x *P. subhirtella*.

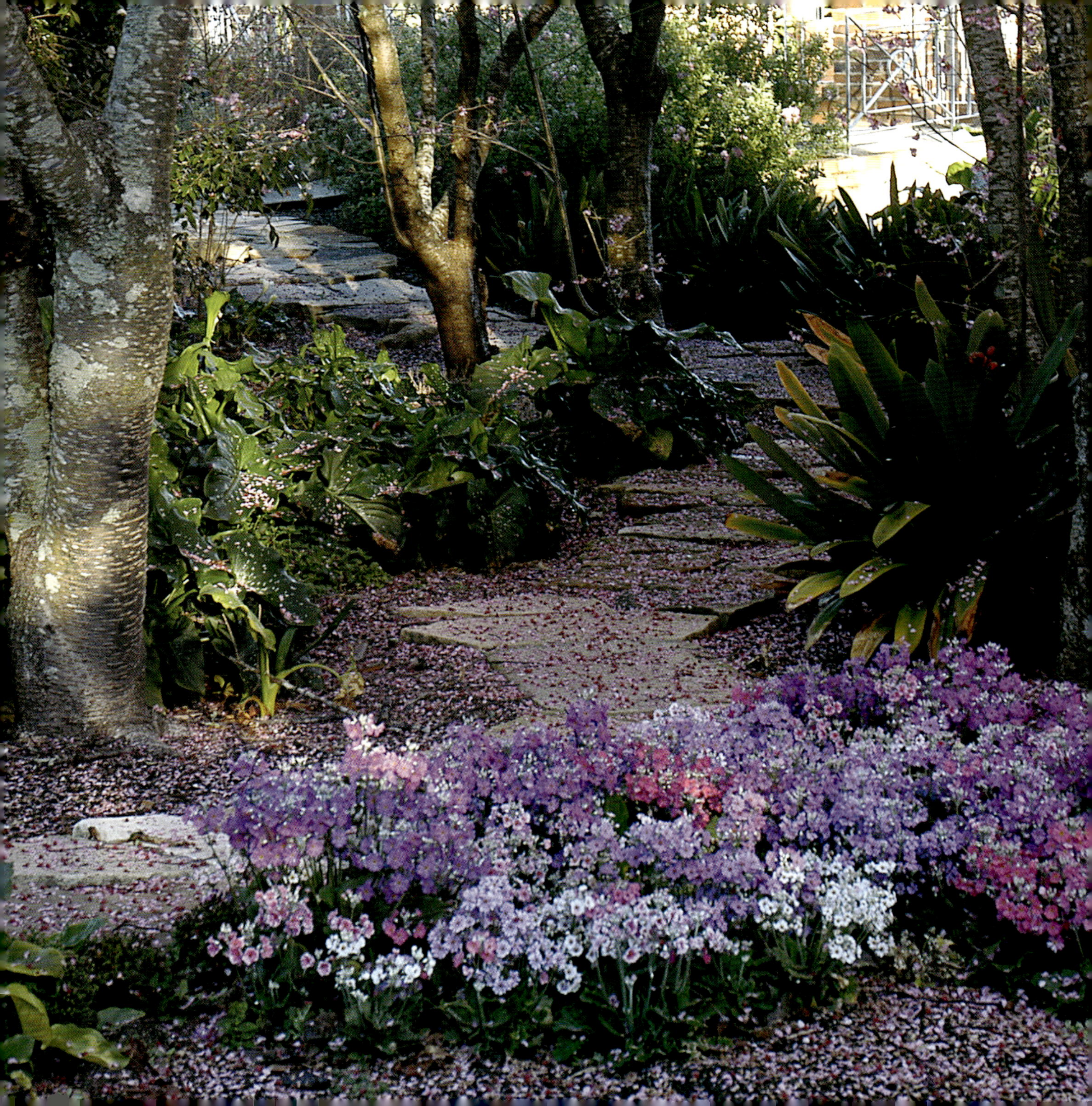

> The delicate soft pink blossom of *Prunus* x 'Blireiana'.

Our best display of cherry blossom blooms around a series of cleverly graded ponds that Bob uses for recycling water from the nursery. At their peak flowering time, the ground surrounding them is carpeted with delicate tiny pink petals. The whole serene scene is captured and framed by looking through what I call our "church window". On a clear day, when the sky is reflected in the blue of the water which is also sprinkled with pink petals, the effect is just exquisite.

My all-time favourite cherry blossom has always been the double soft pink *Prunus* x 'Blireiana'. It has a delicate fragrance reminiscent of almond essence. I was delighted that Bob had several trees of this in the garden because they take me back to my youth. Below my parents' house at Kenton Valley, there were two courts belonging to the local tennis club, where we played most Saturday afternoons. On the adjacent overgrown block, which was part of our farm, there was an old chimney that I loved to ramble around. It was all that remained of the primary school my mother attended in the 1920s. And, lining the entrance driveway to these tennis courts were *Prunus* x 'Blireiana' trees. Nearly every day, when the blossom was out, I broke off a few small branches to decorate my bedroom. I always admired how well the pink blossom contrasted with the lovely grey of the branches.

< *Primula* amongst the falling cherry blossom petals make the loveliest picture.

Graham Ross and Johanna Griggs, from Better Homes and Gardens, filmed the spring opener to their show in our garden in 2008. We had a fantastic day with such a friendly crew and their two great stars.

Trudy watching me photograph the cherry blossom early one spring morning.

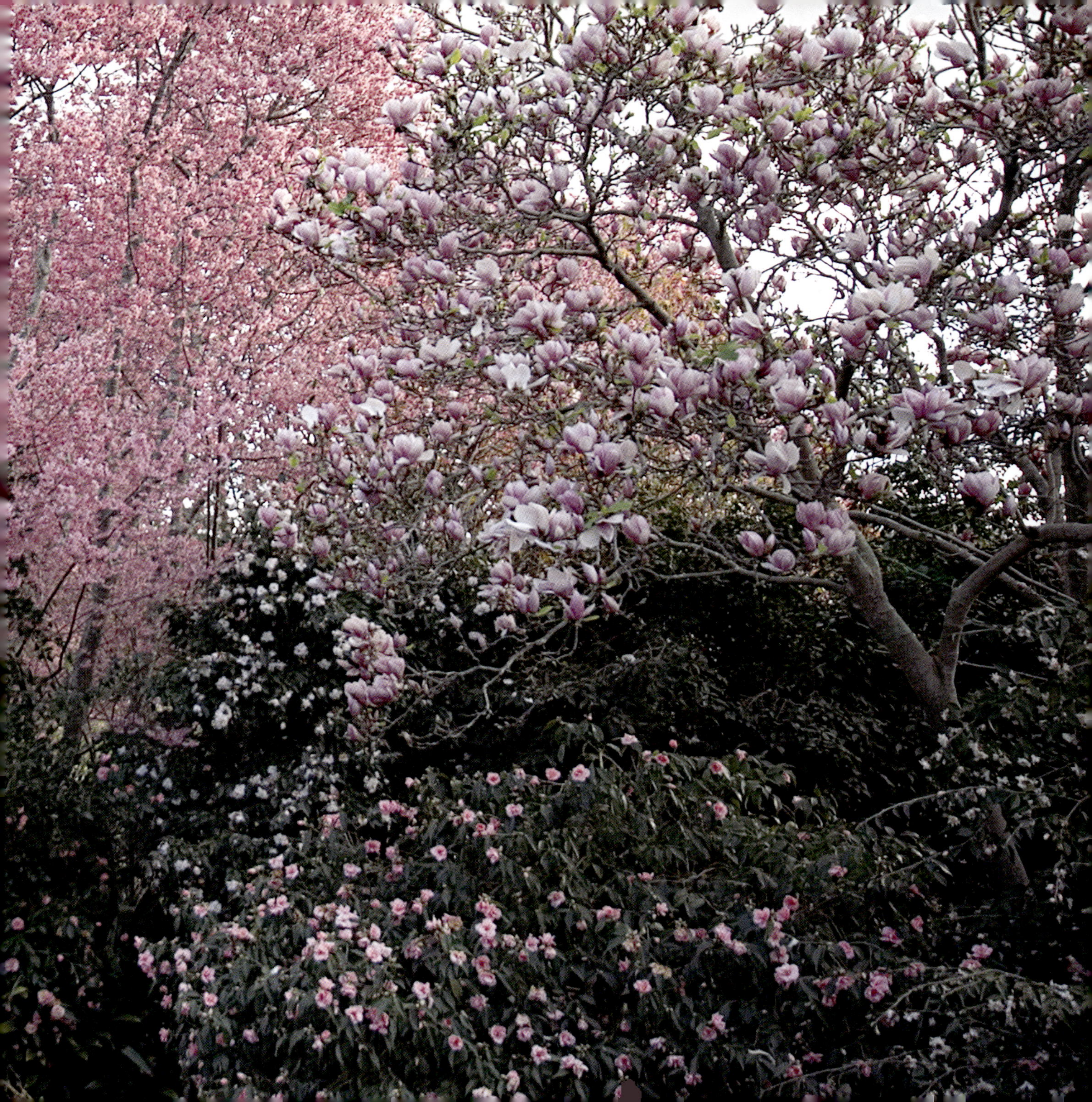

Magnolias in the Mist

Magnolias must have been especially bred for Paradise. They are so divine. Significantly, they are considered to be the oldest known flowering plant in the world, dating back about 93 million years. We have around fifty in the garden – early flowering, mid-flowering and late flowering ones. Pink ones in all shades, white ones, as well as purples and yellows. And on a misty morning, the scene is so incredibly beautiful that you want to freeze it and store it in your mind forever. While I love the amazing, enormous pale-pink blooms of *Magnolia* 'Starwars', there is one variety that outshines the rest – *Magnolia* 'San Jose'. Two stunning specimen trees, planted either side of the driveway, dramatically herald spring's arrival in Paradise. As their magnificent blooms unfold, almost while you watch, from the furry buds along the bare branches, they transform and lighten up the whole garden. From a distance, they almost look like large pink and white confetti covering these amazing trees.

ABOVE L–R: *Magnolia* 'San Jose' blooms are superb; The enormous *Magnolia* 'Starwars' flower is truly spectacular.

On a misty morning in Paradise the magnolias look surreal.

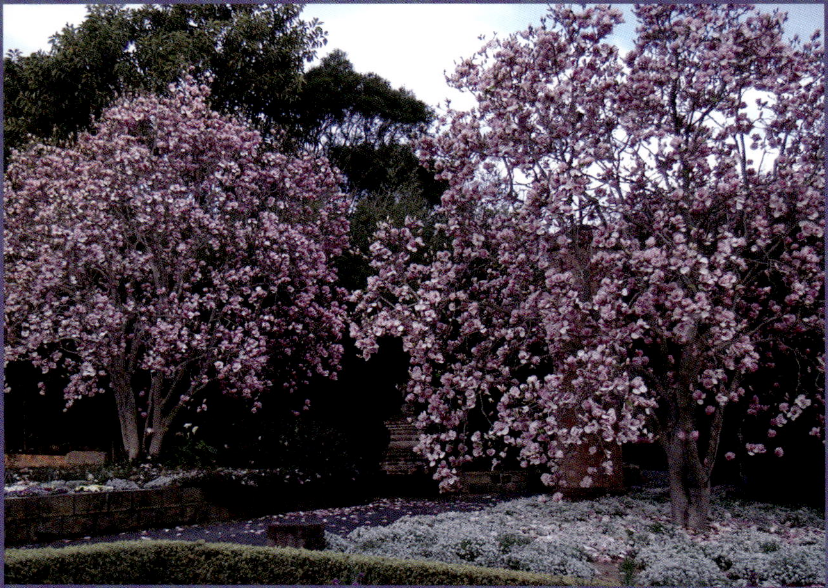

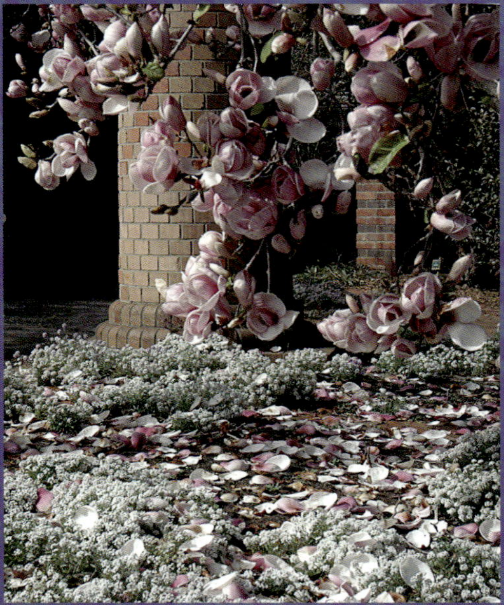

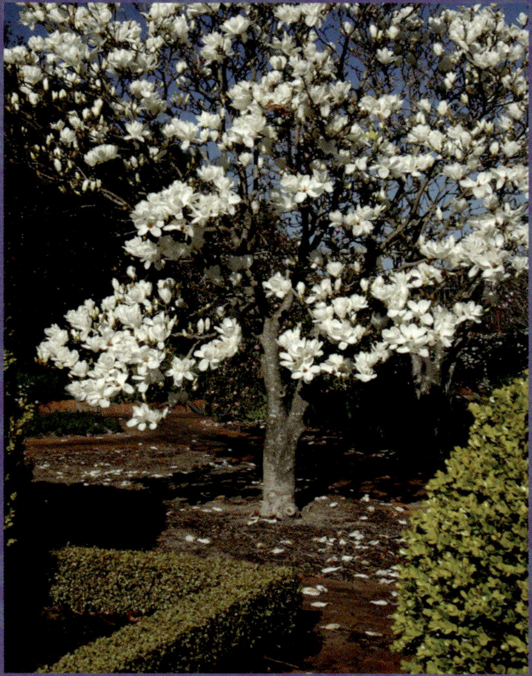

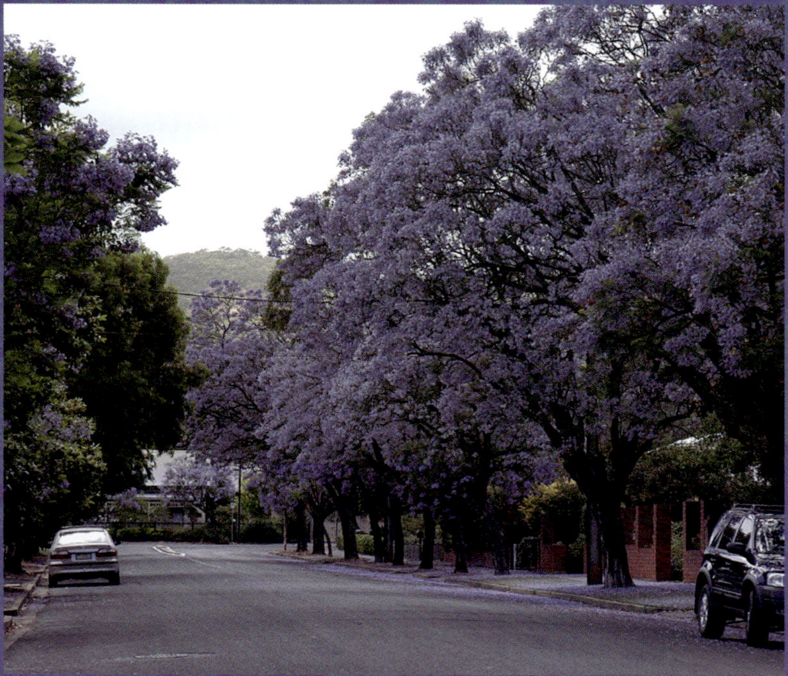

I can still recall my very first encounter with a *Magnolia* – on the edge of Lake Como in Italy, more than thirty years ago. It was April and I jumped out of the car to stand entranced beneath an almighty tree with fabulously huge pale pink flowers. Whatever was it? I had never ever seen anything like it in the environs of Adelaide – or anywhere else for that matter. Bob says it would have been *Magnolia campbellii*.

What garden is complete without a *Jacaranda* tree? They are native to South America, where I have seen them growing along the streets of Buenos Aires. There's something about the colour of *Jacaranda* flowers that lifts one's spirits.

It's the same with the double pink May bush, whose exquisite tiny blossoms seduce me each spring. I am not surprised that it is called *Prunus glandulosa* 'Rosea Plena'. The dainty blossoms are so similar to my favourite *Prunus* x 'Blireiana' blossom. In the tiny outback town of Walcha Road, in northern New South Wales, Bob and I once came across superb bushes of both the single pink and single white May bush growing on the verge outside a very pretty cottage garden. A friendly neighbour assisted us with pruning the specimens ever so lightly, as the owner was away; the cuttings we took are now thriving bushes in Paradise. And the owner was delighted too when we sent her some very special plants in exchange.

Surely, in Paradise, spring must be the most seductive season of all. With a full complement of soothing pastel shades, contrasting with the bright cheery blooms of the thousands of annuals, *Primula*, polyanthus, poppies and pansies that are out at the same time, our garden puts on its very best performance.

< TOP L–R Our twin *Magnolia* 'San Jose' trees make a dramatic entrance to Paradise in spring. Falling *Magnolia* petals look so pretty amongst the white *Alyssum* ground cover.

Jacaranda Blue and the May Bush

v The pristine white blooms of *Magnolia denudata* are a delight to watch as they slowly open.

< BOTTOM L–R *Magnolia denudata* always turns on a magnificent display in August; Fife Avenue in Torrens Park, Adelaide, is lined with *Jacaranda* trees, which are glorious when in full bloom.

Mixed arrangements of 'Alba' and 'Rosea' May bush capture the charm of spring.

A self-sown *Prunus* hybrid.

A common Chinese *Prunus* species.

Prunus cerasoides var. *rubea*, a species from the jungles of western China and Burma.

The tonings in *Prunus persica* 'Versicolor' are so delicate.

The soft pink blossom of *Prunus glandulosa* 'Rosea Plena' (May bush), touched with white, is simply exquisite.

Prunus glandulosa single white form.

Prunus 'Louise Audrey'.

Prunus x 'Blireiana'.

Assorted *Prunus* species that have self-sown in Paradise.

Cabbages look splendid in any vegetable garden, but I was particularly proud of this lot.

Fresh from the Garden

Vegetables are Good for You!

∧ Pre-mulch days when I was trying to create a French potager effect, with flowers and vegetables mixed in together.

"You can't have any dessert until you eat up all your vegetables." For the baby boomers among us, this directive from our parents was the bane of our lives as children. But not for Bob. His mother Audrey has told me he simply would not eat his vegetables; he didn't like desserts either, so there was no incentive she could use to encourage him.

Perhaps that is why, to this day, he only likes digging potatoes. The vegetable garden, which is almost exclusively my domain, is housed within a large rectangular bed about ten metres long and six metres wide, enclosed with wire. Inevitably, with so much room to play in, I got carried away with what I planted there during my early days in Paradise.

How many tedious hours I spent hand-weeding in those first years! But the dogs enjoyed watching me beavering away. They burrowed out a nice hole in the cool earth, sometimes uprooting seedlings in the process, and settled down to watch all the activity. Trudy passed the time by snapping at flies and Jessee liked to have a snooze. On the odd occasion Trudy would go into a frenzy, racing around like she was on fire. I quickly worked out the problem from her symptoms. A bee sting, invariably on one of her paws. So back up to the house we would run to get the Stingose, rubbing it in to ease the pain.

About two years ago, I finally discovered sugar cane mulch! I had been warned that it would attract ants, but that did not deter me. Over several weeks I spread about 30 bales, not only in the vegetable garden, but also in a nearby rose bed. It has been most effective at keeping the weeds under control and eventually I would like it spread over every rose bed.

I overlooked basic economic theory in my early plantings. I painstakingly planted an entire packet of 'Hawkesbury Wonder' dwarf beans, not in the vegetable enclosure this time, but in the chook house. Bob had suggested planting there because of the good work that the chooks were doing in keeping the weeds under control and the ground cultivated. When the new little shoots popped up through the earth, I was fairly pleased with the straight lines I had managed to achieve; but when it came to harvesting, I had a vast oversupply! I did not learn from my mistake, and the next year the same thing happened with my purple and green climbing beans. Baskets and baskets of them went up to the staff lunch room.

> Fortunately I had plenty of cane baskets, some made by my mother, to carry the surplus bean harvest up to the nursery staff.

Mulch, Mulch and Mulch Again!

∧ Resting, after another hard day's work in Paradise.

The Law of Supply and Demand

111

Paradise Pumpkins

This year I have the best pumpkins ever – not for quantity or taste (which still has to be tested), but in appearance! Eleven gigantic bright red-orange pumpkins, which I grew from French seeds purchased at last year's ABC Sydney Gardening Show in Homebush. This heirloom pumpkin dates back several centuries and has an interesting connection to the fairytale "Cinderella", which was written by Charles Perrault in 1697. In illustrations of his story, this wonderful pumpkin was the variety depicted. It turned into the glass coach that took Cinderella to the ball where she met her prince. With all that fascinating history, I have decided to grow these pumpkins every year from now on!

One of the best parts of being involved in gardening shows is seeing what else is on display. Recently I participated in the Bloodtree Festival at Kulnura and ended up bringing home such a pretty little silver-laced Wyandotte chicken. We have named her Sparkle. Her feathers are mostly light grey with a black picotee edge and, at present, she is rather shy. It takes time getting used to new surroundings, let alone new friends. Wyandottes, named after an Indian tribe, were first bred in America in 1883; they now come in a variety of shades, including blues and gold, but the original birds were silver-laced.

Rhubarb and Raspberries

The thought of the colour, let alone taste, of rhubarb and raspberries conjures up images of summer puddings and rhubarb crumble. Yum! In the same way, rosemary, parsley and thyme immediately make me think of roast lamb. "Thought you might like these for the pavlova," says Bob as he hands me a hat full of plump passionfruit plucked from the many vines that he has planted all around the garden. Oranges, lemons and

^ Shaped like huge cheese wheels, my "Cinderella" pumpkins are the French variety 'Rouge Vif d'Etampes'.

< This crop of Paradise pumpkins all sold during one open weekend.

∧ The flowers of the bay tree that we discovered in bloom outside the amazing Baths of Caracalla in Rome.

limes remind me of drinking Campari mixed with fresh orange juice in Spain, as well as one of my favourite drinks, lemon, lime and bitters. And my lemon delicious pudding, using a recipe passed down from my grandmother, has been enjoyed by many guests; they always comment on the lovely bright colour of the lemon sauce.

Plucking bay leaves from our wonderful bay tree, which is about 5 metres high, seems to me such an Italian thing to do. Probably because I once discovered a bay tree, in flower, near the incredible ruins of the ancient Baths of Caracalla, in Rome. These baths, which are Bob's favourite Roman ruins, were built around 212 AD and could

< Italian 'Tuscan Blue' rosemary near our "Stairway to Heaven".

accommodate 1600 people from all classes of society. Having a bath in those times was an outing, much like going to the shopping complexes of today.

It is such a treat to have our own supply of vegetables, herbs, fruit and eggs fresh from the garden. Not only is the produce organic, it is also immensely satisfying to grow your own food.

∧ *Hedychium coccineum* ginger grows wild along our bottom driveway. Unfortunately this variety is only ornamental.

< The beautiful mosaic floor of these Roman baths is still intact in places.

Howard's Way

My twenty years in book publishing involved a lot of eating in restaurants. I never entertained at home much and had certainly never thought about catering en masse. So one day when Bob announced that forty *Camellia* enthusiasts from Victoria were coming to visit the garden and it would be nice to provide lunch for them, I went into a spin. Thank goodness I thought of Howard, who rescued me with his precise instructions over the phone. Our friends Howard Nicholson and Trish Arbib, from Bundanoon Village Nursery, visited us regularly and it was always a delight to talk about food and books with Howard. His collection of books on gardening and plant hunters, food and natural history was well known and he and Trish featured on ABC TV's "Gardening Australia" programme on several occasions.

> Trevor Cochrane, from "The Garden Gurus", munches on an edible *Begonia* that Bob collected in China.

∨ Howard Nicholson also showed me how flowers, such as nasturtiums, could be used to add colour to salads.

Howard's expert and extensive knowledge on all things associated with food was wonderful. I remember him pointing out all the chickweed in my vegetable garden and commenting, "You can use that in salads, you know." His advice on the menu, quantity and preparation, along with numerous other tips, was invaluable, and has been on countless other occasions since that memorable first lunch. Howard passed away in November 2007 and we all miss him terribly. I still have jars of his "Preserved Lime and Date Chutney", and "Damson Chutney", all carefully labelled and dated, in my pantry; one bears an extra handwritten note "Beware stones". Trish continues to run the nursery and has opened a bookshop on the premises as well.

∧ *Citrus medica* var. *sarcodactylus*, otherwise known as Buddha's Hand, decorated with Trish's ring during one of her regular visits to Paradise with Howard.

Christmas bush, on the bottom track, surrounded by gum trees and bracken fern.

On the Wild Side

Shades of the Bush

Every shade of green and brown, with tonings of grey, beige, rust, lemon, caramel, cream and bone mixed in. Those are the colours of our Australian bush. Bob has cleared 25 hectares of his land, but the remainder is pristine bushland. At Paradise we are fortunate to have two creeks, a National Park surrounding us on two sides and natural bush screens on the other boundaries.

In spring the bush lights up, with a succession of mainly red and yellow flowers. Waratahs, which are the symbol of New South Wales, and many *Doryanthes*, or Gymea lilies, whose huge red flower heads are much sought after, both flower profusely. In Paris we once saw a *Doryanthes* flower head on sale in a florist for $2000. Wattles, banksias, grevilleas, and several species of *Persoonia*, which is commonly known as "geebung", also thrive in our bushland. This name derives from the Aboriginal word "jibbong", which indicates that some species have

∧ Signs saying "Beware of falling Bunyas" are often seen in Australian National Parks. Fortunately our Bunya pines are planted off the main track.

> Red-flowering gum, Christmas bush and hydrangeas arranged by Bob for Christmas.

The blossom on the Western Australian red-flowering gum glows a brilliant orange.

> These native orchids grow on the trunks of paperbark trees.

^ Different forms of the Western Australian red-flowering gum, such as this vibrant pink variety, are now available.

> Every tiny bit of gravel on this anthill, shaped like a grave, has been individually carted by an ant from the nearby road surface!

edible fruits; obviously a bush tucker food of old. In fact the whole area around Kulnura abounds in Aboriginal cave paintings, and there are many tool sharpening grooves along the creek beds. The name "Kulnura" actually means "up there in the clouds". How appropriate for the location of a garden called Paradise! Come Christmas, the *Ceratopetalum gummiferum* or Christmas bush makes the prettiest picture, both growing in the wild and picked for arrangements inside the house. Bob is especially proud of the dainty green native orchids, only about 10 cm high, which grow in clusters in the bush near the lake. They are quite a rare species.

∧ Paradise is a haven for *Doryanthes*, which are only found in the Sydney region.

> *Epacris longiflora* has attractive tubular flowers.

Down to the Creek

^ Something in the air catches Trudy's attention, while Jessee is content to just saunter on.

Our creeks are spring-fed and, even in the severest drought, they have never dried up. The track that leads down the gorge to the water is one of the most exciting walks for the dogs. Just before we reach it, Trudy has a last-minute search for the baby wood ducks that have been swimming on the bottom dam. But she gets distracted by the father duck, who deliberately creates a scene by wildly flapping his wings and flying off in the opposite direction.

Halfway down the track the air suddenly changes, and we hear the refreshing sound of running water. The surrounding aromas, such as the pungent native mint, are enhanced. In the heat of summer this is a welcoming place, a cool respite. Majestic blackbutt trees tower high

" *the name Kulnura actually means 'up there in the clouds'* " above the surrounding landscape, and I admire the yellow flowers on *Hibbertia denticulata*, which trail over the rocks. Hanging over the edge of the creek are *Ceratopetalum opetalum* trees, which are commonly known as coachwood or scented satinwood, and in spring there are many Gosford wattles (*Acacia prominens*) flowering all along the edge of the water. Huge staghorns grow on the lillipilly trees.

The bed of the creek is very slippery, as the dogs well know. They tread delicately over the ancient water holes gouged out in the sandstone floor, but even so, one of Jessee's legs goes wobbly. I often choose to sit and meditate, on a wonderful old moss-covered tree that has fallen right across the creek. The dogs find an opening underneath and scramble through to do some more adventuring further upstream. They know I won't be moving for quite a while. I keep hoping that I will spot a platypus in the water but, as Bob has only ever seen two in the creeks, my chances are not great. When we get back to the house it's time to search for leeches on everyone, preferably before paw prints of blood are spread out across the floor.

∧ Hundreds of frogs serenade us at night, including this friendly fellow who took up permanent residence in an *Aspidistra* outside my study.

Paradise on Fire!

For three long days we watched as the fire edged its way towards us up the valley to the south-west. Growing up in the Adelaide Hills gave me a remarkable sense of smell when it comes to bushfires. Just the slightest tinge in the air and I can recognise a fire. It must be fear that has put me on high alert. How well I remember evacuating our house, and taking my prized possession, a beautiful big doll named Sallyann, to the creek; we stayed there for some time in case the encroaching fire came over the hill.

Bob said that he had been waiting for this fire for thirty years and that it had finally arrived. Just in time, the wind changed direction, otherwise we could have lost both the house and the nursery. At the fire's raging peak, we had six fire engines helping out and two helicopters constantly scooping water from our lake. Although our bushland was mostly burnt out, only one plant in the garden was destroyed. It was a *Camellia*.

∨ Watching the reflection of the approaching fire in the windows of the house was a terrifying experience, hopefully never to be repeated!

That fire was started by lightning, something this area is very prone to because of the seams of ironstone that run along the hills and seem to attract it. Rhondda Inchley, who lives in a hilltop retreat up the Yarramalong Valley, told me the following story about an unforgettable flash of lightning. At 3 a.m. one morning, lightning struck a tree just a few metres from her house. She saw a tremendous white flash bounce from the tree to the ground, and her guests at the time were blinded for five minutes afterwards. The next morning she discovered holes, three metres deep, that had been bored into the earth as the lightning sought out the underground cable. When the electrician arrived later, he discovered that the meter box, located *inside* the house, had not only been fried, it had melted! The power of nature is astounding and not to be ignored!

∧ ABOVE L—R The Fire Brigade arrive to save the day, and Paradise; It is extraordinary that the Australian bush can regenerate, within a year, after the devastation caused by fire.

> In the aftermath.

The harmonious colours of our creek bed soothe the soul.

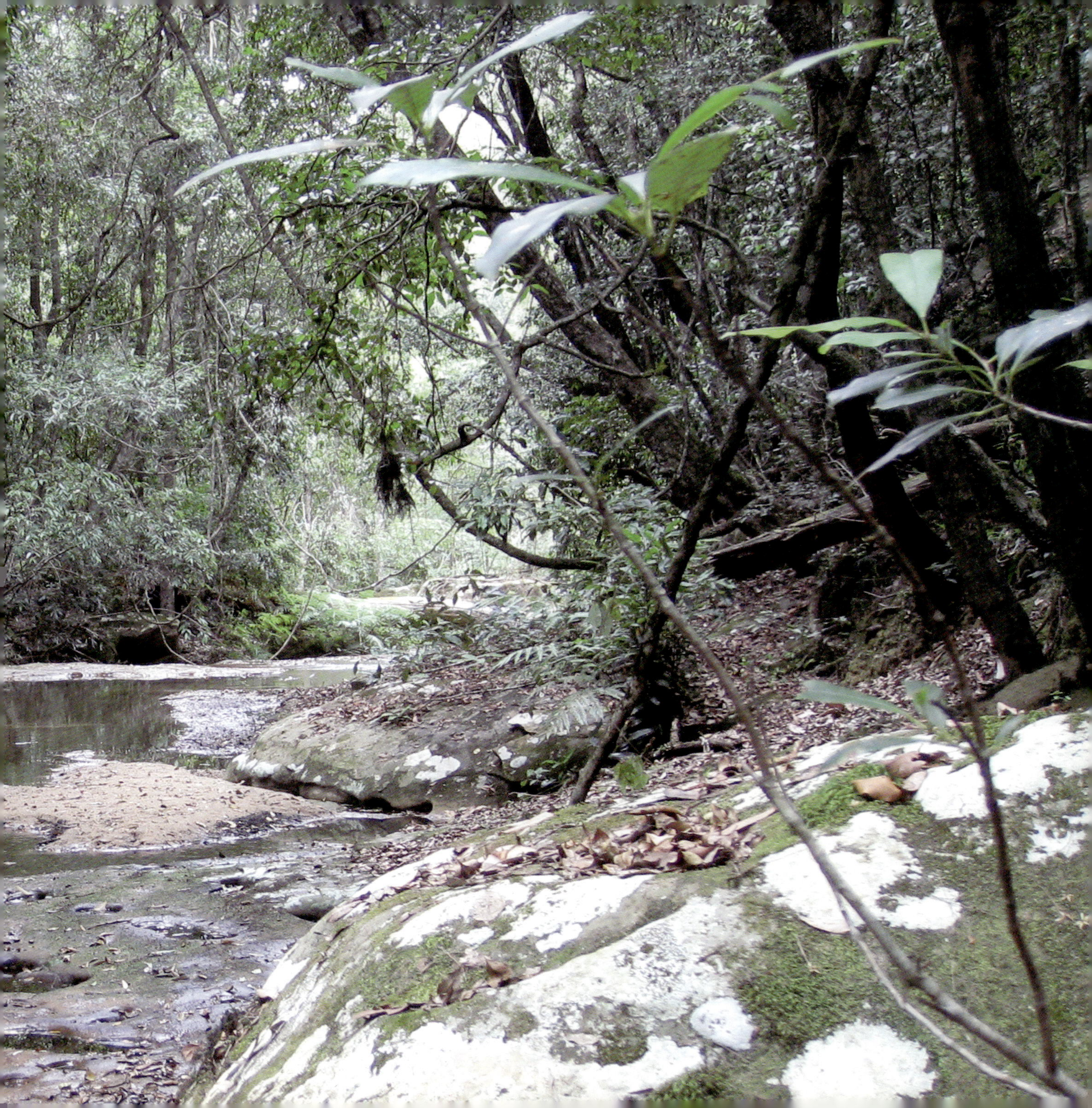

> Waratahs are the floral emblem of New South Wales. It is such a thrill to see them growing in the wild.

Bob's Rainforest by Design

Scattered throughout the garden are numerous rainforest plants, but near the Summer House Bob has created an area exclusively devoted to this theme. Decorative tropical shrubs from China and Vietnam, including the evergreen cherry; trees such as *Eleocarpus* and *Styrax*; and some rare michelias and maples, all mingle happily with ornamental ginger. *Sauravia aspera*, which has lovely corrugated leaves, beautiful pink flowers and sweet edible fruit also thrives here, as do species of *Gardenia* that Bob has introduced to Australia. These rare plants from various countries blend in effectively together to create a shady, tropical atmosphere.

We are proud that living Wollemi pine trees, fossil evidence of which dates back 90 million years, were discovered to the west of us, in the Wollemi National Park. Our tree is growing well near the Summer House, where it can be readily admired by visitors. I can't help wondering what other wonders are waiting to be discovered in our native forests. Perhaps even in Paradise!

< I traced a loud ticking noise to this grasshopper, which had decided to land on my computer.

ABOVE L–R The seed pod on this *Lepidozamia perozkiana* startled our gardener, Jane, when she discovered it by accident. The pods remind me of the mouths of those laughing sideshow clowns, but they could also be some sort of volcanic explosion!; A selection of spring wildflowers makes a charming arrangement, especially the pink *Boronia* which blooms profusely in our bush; The seed pod on this *Lepidozamia communis*, a cycad native to the east coast of New South Wales, is a soft green-grey colour, with a smooth texture almost like velvet.

> The incredible inflorescence on this bangalow palm changes over several months from flower to seed.

The contrast between the pink water lilies and the blue of the lake in front of the house delights all who see it.

Flowers Fantastic

v Cream is the colour most often associated with lotus.

Flower Flights of Fancy

It was only after I had selected the subjects for this vignette that I realised how flowers, just like all the other good things in life (music, food, wine...) can send one off to exotic locations without even having to set foot on a plane. It's all about memories and associations. And so, as this story came together, my mind took off around the world to recall some of my favourite places and countries.

Lotus
China

When I think of lotus, I immediately think of China; I have seen it growing there in tranquil ponds, amongst the serenity of temple grounds, as well as in the countryside. It is one of the most useful and beautiful plants in that country and its rhizomes, tender young leaves and pebble-like seeds are eaten in many dishes. It is also the national flower of India, where Buddhism originated in the 6th century; Buddha is often depicted sitting in the middle of this flower. Ancient Egyptian paintings and frescoes also portray the lotus, whose seeds were in those days used to make flour for bread.

This stunningly beautiful flower grows out of mud. Just a few straggly stalks with huge green leaves appear, and then, seemingly from nowhere, a perfect bud opens to the most fantastic flower. In

< A beautiful new recent addition to our lotus is this shimmering pink shade.

my early days in Paradise I took a magnificent pink and cream bloom to our Kulnura Garden Club meeting. It was about 30 cm wide and, not surprisingly, it won exotic of the month! One year we had so many blooms that I decided to sell the seed pods. They were in great demand as Sydney florists loved using them in their huge commercial floral arrangements, for hotel foyers and the like. We ended up harvesting 2000 pods, and neighbours sold them for us at the Sydney Flower Market. I can still see Bob wading out of the water, clutching a huge bunch. It's not an easy task picking lotus from a canoe! We also lost our best pair of Swiss Felco secateurs overboard.

Although lotus mainly flower in pink, white and cream, there are other colours and shades which grow in India that I would like to obtain, especially the large double deep pink variety, *Nelumbo nucifera*. And I have recently heard the exciting news that blue and yellow varieties of lotus have been bred in Hawaii. Just imagine how beautiful a true blue lotus, set amongst pink water lilies, would look! In Paradise, our lotuses flower for about two months each year, starting in the middle of December.

^ A perfect lotus bud about to unfold.

I associate water lilies with Claude Monet and my mind goes straight to the Orangerie Museum in Paris where his magnificent water lily paintings are on display. Wrapped around the walls in delicious curves, they are unforgettably magic in shades of blue, pink, green and mauve, with highlights of cream, yellow and white.

Water Lilies
France

< Trudy and Jessee enjoy swimming amongst the water lily leaves!

> Water lilies are like bright magic stars.

Yellow and pink blooms proliferate in the middle pond, but the lake in front of our house also has whites, blues, purples and darker shades of pink. Some come out at different times of the day, although most of the yellows flower all day. At night, they all close their waxy petals, to reopen again the next day and for several days to come. It is amusing watching our water hens using the many water lily leaves as stepping stones, especially while they are building nests and carrying flowers in their beaks. Not quite like the five-foot-wide leaves of the giant Amazon water lily, *Victoria amazonica*, which shot to fame in England in 1849 when Joseph Paxton stood his seven-year-old daughter on one of the leaves. Paxton, who was Head Gardener at Chatsworth, had successfully flowered this species in England for the first time in his glass conservatory.

"I owe having become a painter to flowers"   CLAUDE MONET

Worsleya
Brazil

"Is the *Worsleya* out yet?" our friend, Sue Entwhistle asks at regular intervals from late November onwards. By mid-December it is just coming out in all its glory. Leo Schofield gave Bob some seeds about ten years ago. It is notoriously difficult to grow, so they were both delighted that three magnificent plants resulted. With leaves like soft green blades on a scythe, protruding from a stalk about one metre high, their glory unfolds into a spidery multiple flower head, lavender blue, the size of a large dinner plate. Mostly one, sometimes two, flower heads per plant. This is one flower that I would never dream of picking – it looks so majestic in the garden.

It was fascinating to learn that *Worsleya procera* or *Worsleya rayneri* (apparently it was named twice!) originates from South America, where its common names are Empress of Brazil and blue amaryllis. Even more incredible, it is now nearly extinct in the wild and came from only one ridge in the mountains south east of Rio de Janeiro. And here it is thriving in our garden! I can't help conjuring up images of some of the exotic parrots of South America, such as the magnificent blue and gold macaw and the arrestingly strange yet beautiful toucan with its enormous beak, gliding through the rainforest. As indeed I once saw in Brazil. That colourful country is also famed for its rich holdings of semi-precious stones, such as amethyst, rose quartz, topaz and emerald. It seems so appropriate that this stunning plant comes from such an exotic location.

< *Worsleya rayneri* is crowned with such a splendid, majestic flower head.

Belladonna Lilies
England

Part of the Amaryllis family, *Amaryllis belladonna* is actually native to South Africa. Commonly called Easter lily, it has also acquired the name "naked ladies", because the flowers appear before the leaves – but I like to think it is because they are reminiscent of perfect pink English complexions. The flowers begin to appear in mid to late January, in shades of pale pink, bright pink, cream and white; some blooms are both pink and white.

< Bob's arrangement of *Amaryllis belladonna* was just right in our new vase from the Blue Mountains.

> This miniature *Cymbidium*, called 'Chianti', was grown by my father; it spills out gracefully from our Iranian water jug made of pewter.

< Green cymbidiums, with a red lip, were my father's favourite – and they are now Bob's too.

Bob loves his native orchids in the scrub in Paradise, but for me the *Cymbidium* is hard to surpass. What other flower will last in a vase for two months? They save me a lot of work over winter, as I usually arrange five large vases of sprays in the house for the August open weekend. They last right through until September – without me even needing to change the water! On occasion, I have even brought whole plants, sometimes with ten spikes on each, and placed them in our entrance foyer for about two months. What a spectacle they make to greet our visitors at the front door!

Orchids
Singapore

> White cymbidiums were originally my favourite orchids and they possibly still are.

It is amazing that the intricate pattern on each *Cymbidium* flower has hardly any variation.

The fleur-de-lys was the symbol of the French monarchy before the revolution, but I associate irises more with the famous painting by Vincent Van Gogh. Fabulous new varieties are being bred at Rainbow Ridge Nursery near Orange in New South Wales.

> Sadly, Paradise is too warm to grow these Japanese *Iris*, which rank amongst the most desirable.

Agapanthus
Greece

As the word "agape" is Greek for love, and "anthos" translates as flower in Greek, you would think *Agapanthus* were native to Greece. But no, they actually originate from South Africa. This flower was first discovered in 1679, but it was not until 1789 that it was called *Agapanthus* by L'Heritier, a Frenchman. It is still a mystery as to why he gave this flower a Greek name, but I have my own theory. I think it must have reminded him of the perfect blue of the Aegean Sea. Just think of the Greek Islands, dotted with white buildings around the little harbours. Even the Greek flag is blue and white!

Our many clumps of *Agapanthus* peek out from amongst groves of camellias and look splendid in front of sandstone walls. At Christmas, bright blue, some even tinged lavender, and white *Agapanthus* complement the red and blue tablecloths from Provence that I set out, providing the perfect contrast to the many red Chinese lanterns that adorn our ceiling during the festive season. *Agapanthus* fit into my category of fantastic flowers because they are such an extraordinary clear blue colour and have such a unique appearance.

The petals of the *Agapanthus* are displayed so very prettily.

∨ White *Agapanthus* are always useful for landscaping white-themed gardens.

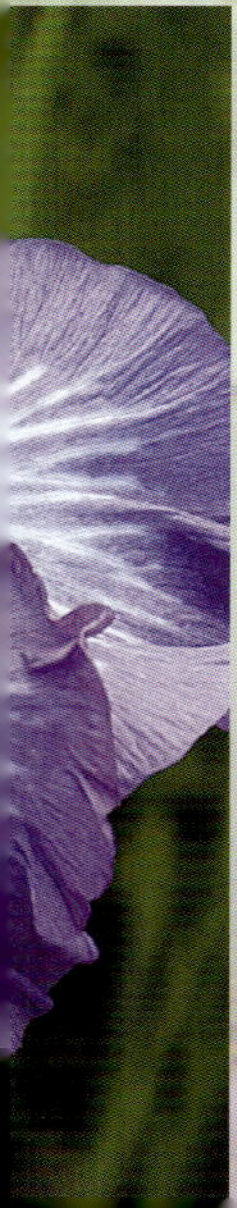

Bird of Paradise
New Guinea

For flamboyancy, it is hard to beat the peculiar *Strelitzia nicholai*. Now we are in New Guinea, where magnificent plumes from birds of paradise are woven into the most amazing arrangements for chiefs to wear on their heads during sing-sing celebrations. My first ever overseas trip was to New Guinea, at the end of 1971, when I participated in a village exchange scheme organised through the university at Port Moresby. For part of the three months that I was there, I stayed in a small village called Banz. It was near Mount Hagen in the Highlands, and I shared a hut with one of the chief's wives. Of his ten wives, only three were still alive. It was a time of incredible excitement. Pink Floyd were recording their album "Obscured by Clouds", which was inspired by the wilds of New Guinea – especially the song "La Vallée" – but the country was still considered too remote for most people. The day I walked miles and miles over mountains and down valleys to see a sing-sing is etched in my memory. Four-hundred people turned up, but I was the only white person – and I had just turned nineteen! The thrill of these raw mountains and remote places, and the challenge of finding something new, still excites me when I travel with Bob – and I know it is just the same for him.

< This display of *Strelitzia nicholai*, commonly known as bird of paradise was arranged by our voluntary ikebana group.

v The similarity between these gondolas outside the Ducal Palace in Venice and *Strelitzia nicholai* flowers is uncanny.

∧ The chief and one of his wives were delighted to have this picture taken after they had adorned me with *Hibiscus* and poinsettia blooms, and a crown made with bird of paradise plumes.

Hibiscus
Hawaii

When I was about four years old, I often picked the prettiest frilly double pink flower from our garden during summer. Sadly, it would only last a day in water – by the morning it was all shrivelled up. But I discovered that if you added a little sugar to the water, you could extend the life of this flower by one whole extra day! The reason I now rank *Hibiscus* among my flowers fantastic is the incredible range and variety available today. Years ago, when I came up to Sydney twice a year for book publishing sales conferences, I remember being amazed to see yellow *Hibiscus* in the gardens of the waterfront properties at Palm Beach, one of Sydney's wealthy northern suburbs.

The yellow *Hibiscus* is the national flower of Hawaii. One species, *Hibiscus mutabilis*, appears throughout China, enhancing the landscape wherever it grows, even on the side of dusty village roads. Its blooms are unique for three different colours: pale pink, mid-pink and white flowers all appear on the same bush. Not surprisingly in China, where everything seems to have multiple uses, *Hibiscus* is used to make many things, including tea and cosmetics. We are acquiring a collection of *Hibiscus* here in Paradise, which I try to add to each year when we visit Queensland. Much to my delight, they were recently given their very own bed.

< TOP *Hibiscus* flowers have such a pleasing shape. CENTRE *Iris* was a Greek Goddess who appeared in rainbows, which were thought to connect heaven and earth. This *Iris* is appropriately named 'Chasing Rainbows'. BOTTOM Orange stamens set off this frilly pink *Hibiscus* bloom.

∧ This *Amaranthus* popped up of its own accord near the house and turned out to be a real beauty!

∧ In Mexico, *Amaranthus* seed is used as a grain food source.

< I collected this starfish when I lived in New Zealand. Its similarity in shape to the *Amaranthus* is quite remarkable.

'Mister Lincoln', 'Charles de Gaulle', 'Fiona's Wish', and 'Old Fragrance' feature, amongst others, in another pewter vase from Iran.

A Bucket of Roses

Down the Garden Path

As I stoop to pick another red rose, a wonderful feeling of peace sweeps over me. It is late November and the welcome rain has stopped falling. Everything is fresh and lovely and the newly opened blooms are exquisite. A frog croaks in the background and nearby a bird sings its evening serenade. The elegant long dark-red buds of 'Mister Lincoln' are perfect for picking and will open in a day or so, eventually fading to a plummy purple colour. 'Roundelay' is coming into its second flush for the year and its velvety red flowers look superb. I add some pink-tinged lavender 'Paradise' and lilac 'Charles de Gaulle' roses and stand back to admire my collection. And once again I reflect how picking roses in the cool of the evening is one of my greatest pleasures.

Lingering in the fading light, with my cut roses gently resting in a bucket of water, I decide to continue dead-heading. It's a scenario I play out most evenings in the summer months when my roses are in full bloom. Through constant dead-heading, I can sometimes achieve seven rose flushes from October through to April, especially on 'Bonica'. The reward for my efforts is always the same – a bucket or two of roses. I have plenty of roses to choose from – at last count there were 1150 bushes of all shapes and sizes growing in our garden. Often I have up to sixteen vases in the house, some filled with fifty or more blooms. Their fragrance wafts throughout the rooms and their beauty enthralls everyone who enters our front door. Perhaps I too have a link with the ancient Romans, who celebrated their festive occasions by decorating

> 'Simply Magic' is a floribunda rose, released in France by Meilland in 1993, that continually produces masses of huge flower heads.

everything with roses. One of the roses they used, the pink and white *Rosa canina*, was also used to treat rabies. Not that I have ever made a carpet of roses, as Cleopatra did for Marc Antony. And I have yet to add their fresh petals to my bath, although the notion is tempting!

"Right then, off we go," I instruct the dogs and we set off along the ever familiar paths. Up the driveway a little, then left to Mother's garden, past the row of low growing salmon-pink 'Simply Magic', up around the corner and right past the bed of 'Bazaar', back down to the main driveway and along until we reach the picking garden. Many a time, by this stage, Trudy and Jessee have decided to either take a detour through the nursery or play with our water dragon lizards, which endlessly tantalize and tease them. Often these cheeky creatures will pose less than a metre away from the dogs, only to escape at the very last minute by leaping through the air or diving into the pond metres below. Then down the hill to the trial beds. Because some rose varieties are more susceptible to diseases such as mildew and black spot, we like to trial them in this bed; we do not spray our roses. Finally we wind our way back to the house, passing another two rose beds near the *Wisteria* pergola.

At breakfast the next morning, Bob comments: "A bunch of pink roses mixed in with the last of the blue and mauve larkspurs would be nice in our new vase." By 7.30 a.m. the dogs and I are out again amongst the roses. We have just returned from a couple of weeks away, driving down to my home town of Adelaide. En route we picked up yet another vase from the Victory Theatre Antique Centre at Blackheath in the Blue Mountains. It will make a useful addition to our collection from around the world. Made in England in the 1950s, it is pale

∧ Mixed arrangements of different roses look appealing in our vase from Tavistock in England. You can make your own flower preservative with equal parts of lemon juice, bleach and sugar.

Early the Next Morning

blue, embossed with sprays of daisies, and about 26 cm high. Looped handles on either side add to its charm.

This morning, lovely blooms on the musk scented shell-pink 'The Children's Rose' have opened and there are slender buds of the silvery pink 'Violina' ready for plucking. Overnight a lovely spray of the prettiest pale pink 'Savoy Hotel' has unfolded and I cannot resist some splendid romantic dark crimson 'Fisherman's Friend'. This regal David Austin rose has the most dreadful thorns but its glorious perfume is incomparable.

Golden Memories

Strolling along the paths, I spy a cluster of golden blooms peeking out at me. It's 'Victoria Gold', which was bred by the late Eric Welsh. Each Melbourne Cup Day you see masses of it in full bloom around the race course. What a legacy to leave behind. Eric was a great friend of Bob's. Roses evoke such poignant memories and associations. This morning I think about when Bob first took me to see Eric's rose garden at Erina. He had sprayed his plants with a new fungicide and they were not looking at all healthy. Nevertheless we enjoyed a cup of tea and a good chat. He was delighted when I told him I had planted the pretty pink 'Megan Louise' in our garden. Named in 1981 after one of his daughters who died in her twenties, it was very special.

Bob had just removed a large *Camellia* from a small triangular bed. He continually claims that whenever I see some bare earth, in goes a rose behind his back. So I seized this opportunity to make a garden with my mother's favourite roses – 'Peace', the thornless and very early flowering 'First Love', 'Chicago Peace', 'Fragrant Plum' and, nearby, three 'City of Adelaide' bushes. A shrub version of 'Pinkie' is just along the path. In Adelaide, at the end of a lane near where my parents lived

< Roses will forever be associated with sentiment, as portrayed in this Italian statue.

The last of the larkspurs, in the background, blend in well with the blue and lavender shades of Lobelia *and violas.*

in Torrens Park, grew the best example of a climbing 'Pinkie' that I have ever seen. Smothered in blooms, it put on a fabulous display each year that spanned about six metres square.

And when I see our sweetly scented *Dianthus* growing under roses, I remember the silvery pale pink buds and blooms of 'First Love' underplanted with the pretty clove-scented cerise *Dianthus* 'Mrs Gullens' growing right in front of my bedroom window at Kenton Valley in the Adelaide Hills. In that garden, where I spent my teenage years, we grew 200 roses. And each Friday, after school, I would delight in inspecting the magnificent huge rose arrangements that my mother had spent hours preparing just for me!

Each time I pick a rose, I trim off most of the leaves. I have discovered a trick to avoid their thorny stems by simply grasping them by their necks. It works every time. Birds twitter away and tiny superb Sydney blue wrens hop around with gay abandon. One surviving patch of larkspurs has enough blooms for my vase. The colours of these 'fairy flowers' are truly beautiful. Some are dark blue, and others mauve through to pale pink shades and bright clear blue. There is even a pure white. Trudy is by my side as we enter the house. Once inside, she looks at me lovingly with her soulful eyes: "Mum, I'm all wet, please

A stunning display of 'Versigny' in The Heritage Garden. This rose was released by Guillot in 1998.

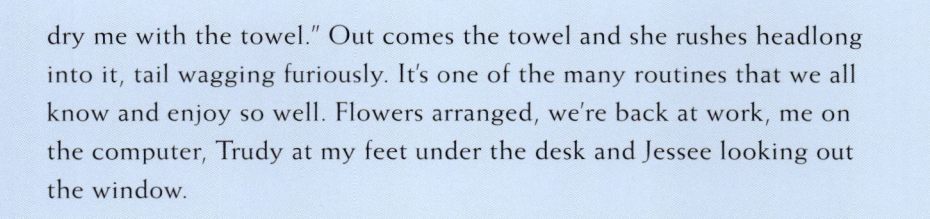

dry me with the towel." Out comes the towel and she rushes headlong into it, tail wagging furiously. It's one of the many routines that we all know and enjoy so well. Flowers arranged, we're back at work, me on the computer, Trudy at my feet under the desk and Jessee looking out the window.

I had wanted to see Walter Duncan's garden of roses near Clare for several years, and the trip to Adelaide seemed to be my opportunity at last. Amongst my copious files on roses was a catalogue from his nursery. What attracted my attention was the inclusion of new French roses from a breeder called Guillot, who I had never heard of.

Walter Duncan Roses

> Bob admiring the beautiful beds of French Guillot roses in Walter Duncan's garden near Clare in South Australia.

And the heading on the first page of this 2003 catalogue: 'Three stunning new varieties fresh from France'. I discovered that Walter had made a new garden, called The Heritage Garden, at Sevenhill a few kilometres out of Clare. I booked an early visit with Walter's wife, Kay, as she had a group of ladies arriving at 11 a.m. I did not want to hold her up as I know what a nuisance just two people can be, wandering around and asking questions, when a large group arrives at the same time.

The morning of our visit dawned with a perfect blue sky, not too hot. The Duncans' gracious old bluestone villa looked gorgeous set amidst beds of roses at their peak. Later on, Walter told us that it was actually a new house made of old materials recycled from his father's house in Adelaide. It was not long before I found the

> A climbing yellow rose sets off a bluestone cottage in the Adelaide Hills town of Mount Torrens.

< It is easy to see the similarity between roses and cherry blossom.

French rose beds. They were beyond belief – without a doubt they were the best roses I have ever seen in Australia. For growth, colour, perfume, shape of bush and form of bloom: on all scores they were simply the best. I was thrilled when Bob agreed with me. As we strolled down near the house, Walter approached us and introduced himself. After he discovered my passion for roses, we spent the next couple of hours enjoying each and every rose bush in his garden; I left with the names of the very best Guillot roses. As Walter no longer has a nursery, I needed to know where to buy them. "Knights Nursery at Gawler," he told me, and I have since placed my order for 100 plants for delivery next winter. When Bob casually mentioned the other day "I'm taking out all those plants and trees over there at the back of the barbecue house. That should make some nice rose beds," I responded in a flash: "That's where the Guillot roses can go!" And we plan to visit their nursery in France later this year!

Fortuitously, I even managed to buy several plants on the way home from Adelaide. At Treloar Roses near Portland in Victoria, I purchased two 'Sonia Rykiel' (named after the French fashion designer), one 'Paul Bocuse' (to honour the French chef from Lyon) and one 'Martine Guillot'. I wanted to start growing them in our garden as soon as possible. After only a couple of weeks in the ground, 'Sonia Rykiel' has already showed her glorious pink globular flowers, 'Paul Bocuse' his blend of apricot shades and 'Martine Guillot' her creamy white. All of them have very double blooms and the most intense fragrance. I cannot contain my excitement for future massed beds of them here at Paradise. Especially lots of 'William Christie', which made such a pretty pink border in the Duncans' sumptuous garden.

^ This fabulous new Guillot rose, as yet unnamed, will be released in Australia in 2010.

> The lovely apricot tonings of the intensely fragrant 'Paul Bocuse', released by Guillot in 1997.

< A perfect bloom of the exquisite Guillot rose 'Chantal Merieux'.

v Our bed of young 'Centenaire de Lourdes' contrasts well with 'Bonica' in the foreground.

Since seeing these roses growing in South Australia, I have been even more fascinated to learn that the Guillot family have bred roses since 1834. And that in 1867 they bred the famous 'La France', which has been designated as the very first hybrid tea rose in the world. Furthermore they bred the world's first polyantha rose, white 'Ma Pâquerette', in 1875. What a claim to fame! Now located near Lyon in central France, they call their range Rosa Générosa, which they define as "new roses which combine the charm and diversity of the old roses with the qualities of modern roses". So we can expect lots of fragrant blooms that continue flowering throughout the season.

Guillot claim that roses can develop scents like "violets, apple, banana and lilies of the valley". Robert Calkin worked in the perfume industry, and with David Austin for many years, developing new fragrances. We met him one summer at a garden party held by the Royal National Rose Society at White House Farm, which is located at Ivy Hatch near Sevenoaks in Kent. At the time we were staying with our friends Rosemary and Maurice Foster, who own this beautiful rose garden filled with hundreds of old-fashioned roses. I learnt a lot about fragrance in roses on that occasion. They vary so much – from spices, to nearly all fruits, honey, watercress, almond, cloves and even "green" notes such as cut grass and cucumber! What I also remember about this lovely day was when a very stylish Count and Countess arrived from Belgium. They had just stepped off the plane and were carrying the first luscious cherries of the season in two small straw baskets. Having read that cherries are part of the Rosaceae family, I cannot resist questioning Bob about this very interesting fact. "Cherry, apple, peach and crab-apple, as well as strawberry, blackberry and raspberry are all in the rose family," he replies. It's not such a surprise after all that roses can produce such a variety of fragrances!

∧ 'Citron Fraise', another Delbard released in 1998, has the colourings of lemon and strawberry.

< The hybrid tea 'Henri Matisse' was released by Delbard in 1995. Its cerise petals, splashed and striped with raspberry and pink shades, are quite superb.

∧ *R. banksiae* 'Lutea' is a lovely lemon shade.

∧ 'Centenaire de Lourdes' was released by Delbard in France in 1958.

A French Love Affair

My love affair with French roses goes back many years. Not only to when I lived in Paris in 1977 but more recently, in 2002, when I discovered that a range of Delbard roses was being imported into Australia for the first time. That year these roses, new to Australia, were launched at the Melbourne International Flower Show. The stand was decked out as a French café, and masses of one glorious bright-pink rose tumbled from silver buckets in a border right along the front. Of course I fell in love with them instantly. My favourite colour and country combined, and at the end of the show I purchased eight plants of this gorgeous pink rose, 'Centenaire de Lourdes', from the display. They now thrive in a bed of their own – with one 'Nahema' keeping them company. The essence from this exquisite silky sugar-pink rose is used by Guerlain in manufacturing their perfume 'Nahema'. This sweetly scented rose is also a popular choice for bridal bouquets in Europe – and I can understand why. It has an ethereal quality about it, mainly because of its delicate colour and divine fragrance.

One of my favourite rose gardens in the world also happens to be French. The Roseraie du Val-de-Marne, in the Paris suburb of L'Haÿ-les-Roses, dates back to 1899 and is one of the largest and most historically important rose gardens in Europe. It is designed in the shape of a huge triangle and its 15,000 massed rose bushes, and the fantasy of arches and trellises covered in roses, make it a must to visit for rosarians. The only criticism that Bob had about this garden was that its arches were too low. With a bit of extra height they would have looked even better. He stood next to them so that we could accurately record the dimensions in photographs.

On our first visit to this garden, Bob made an exciting discovery. We had recently bought a rose from Benefield's Rose Farm at Halfway

∧ The polyantha rose we called Grafton Pink – Bob identified it as 'Raymond Privat' in Paris.

< I fell in love with 'Laure Davoust', a multiflora rose dating back to 1834, when I first saw it growing at L'Haÿ-les-Roses.

Creek near Grafton. It had been given to Pat Benefield and as he was unable to identify it, we just called it Grafton Pink. Walking around the paths between all the beds in this amazing French rose garden, I saw Bob seriously examining one polyantha rose. It was 'Raymond Privat', which was released in 1935. Identified as a mauve colour, it had exactly the same growth habit and flower as our Grafton Pink. Except that our rose was more mauve fading into pink shades, which could be explained by it being washed out by our harsher sun. The best thing about this rose is that it flowers all year round.

Walking under roses seems to cast a special charm. To enter our King's Garden, you pass under clusters of the romantic soft silvery pink 'Blossomtime' and the bright clear pink blooms of 'Zephirine Drouhin'. 'Blossomtime' has a special association for me. It reminds me of Betty Long, who lived in her own home in Torrens Park, Adelaide until she died at the age of 94. So many times, on my visits to Adelaide to see my mother, we walked around to Betty's place. And always the talk would revolve around what was new in her garden. Or what was looking just perfect at that moment. Or how hard it was trying to find yellow and white violas to plant in her wheelbarrow. But she would keep on searching, as she was determined to have those colours in her garden that year!

Betty called her picturesque cottage and garden next to Brownhill Creek her "paradise". How interested she would have been to know that I now lived in another Paradise.

∧ 'Blossomtime' blooms are perfect in this blue jug from Gloucester in England.

∧ Clockwise from bottom left: 'Centenaire de Lourdes', 'Roundelay' and 'The Fairy', with a touch of 'Paradise' complement the English vase that we bought in New Zealand.

'Blossomtime' was one of her favourite roses and it was in her garden that I first saw its delicate blooms growing on a wooden trellis by the side of her driveway. If she wasn't gardening, Betty was busy indulging in her other love in life – baking. Many a time my mother and I arrived home to discover a spectacularly high sponge cake, smothered in fresh cream, sitting on the verandah by our front door. Or occasionally a loaf of freshly made bread at our back door. Although there was no note, we always knew where these goodies came from!

Because we have such a large garden with plenty of space, Bob likes to work on a large scale for maximum impact. One arch he designed soars more than six metres high and four metres wide and becomes covered with the tiny blooms of the sweet double pale-pink climbing rose 'Cécile Brunner'. I am always disappointed that this rose does not bloom for longer. Even its repeat flowers seem fairly sparse. But I would never remove it. It is a sport of the original 'Cecile Brunner', released by Ducher in France in 1881, which was often called the Sweetheart Rose. It reminds me of that Victorian era as it would have been the perfect rose to put in one's buttonhole or arrange in one's hair. Another pergola, about 20 metres long, 4 metres wide and 5 metres high, is our *banksiae* rose walk. When it is covered in double pale yellow, double white and single yellow flowers from several different bushes, it makes a stunning feature in our garden.

On our recent trip to Adelaide, we passed through Clarendon in the Adelaide Hills. The bakery there proved a delight as it was filled with German pastries and cakes. But even more exciting was the small nursery we found behind a stone cottage. Bushes of 'Bonica' about five feet tall, in full bloom, made a gorgeous hedge facing the road; and on the side wall of the house, facing the driveway, was one of the most beautiful apricot-shaded frilly edged roses that I have ever seen. I discovered it was 'Twilight Glow' – another must-have French rose, bred by Meilland in 1991. Travelling home over the next week, I planned out what rose improvements to make on my return. To start with I badly needed to trim back the climbers that were spreading wildly all over our chicken house. 'Albertine' is lovely but only blooms for a few weeks and its repeat blooms are scarcely worth the effort. I decided that the big sprawling bush Bob had intended to use as understock had to go. It was strangling the climbers behind it. When I finally got around to attacking it, I was surprised to find a label in front of one of the climbers. It was 'Twilight Glow'. When or where I bought it, I simply cannot recall!

∧ Pretty in pink, my first great niece Charlize Ella Horbelt. I hope she will love roses as much as I do!

> My grandmother's Victorian dressing table set is the prettiest I have seen.

159

It is interesting that the colour scheme in the Roseraie du Val-de-Marne is mostly pinks, purples and whites, as shown in this arched walkway.

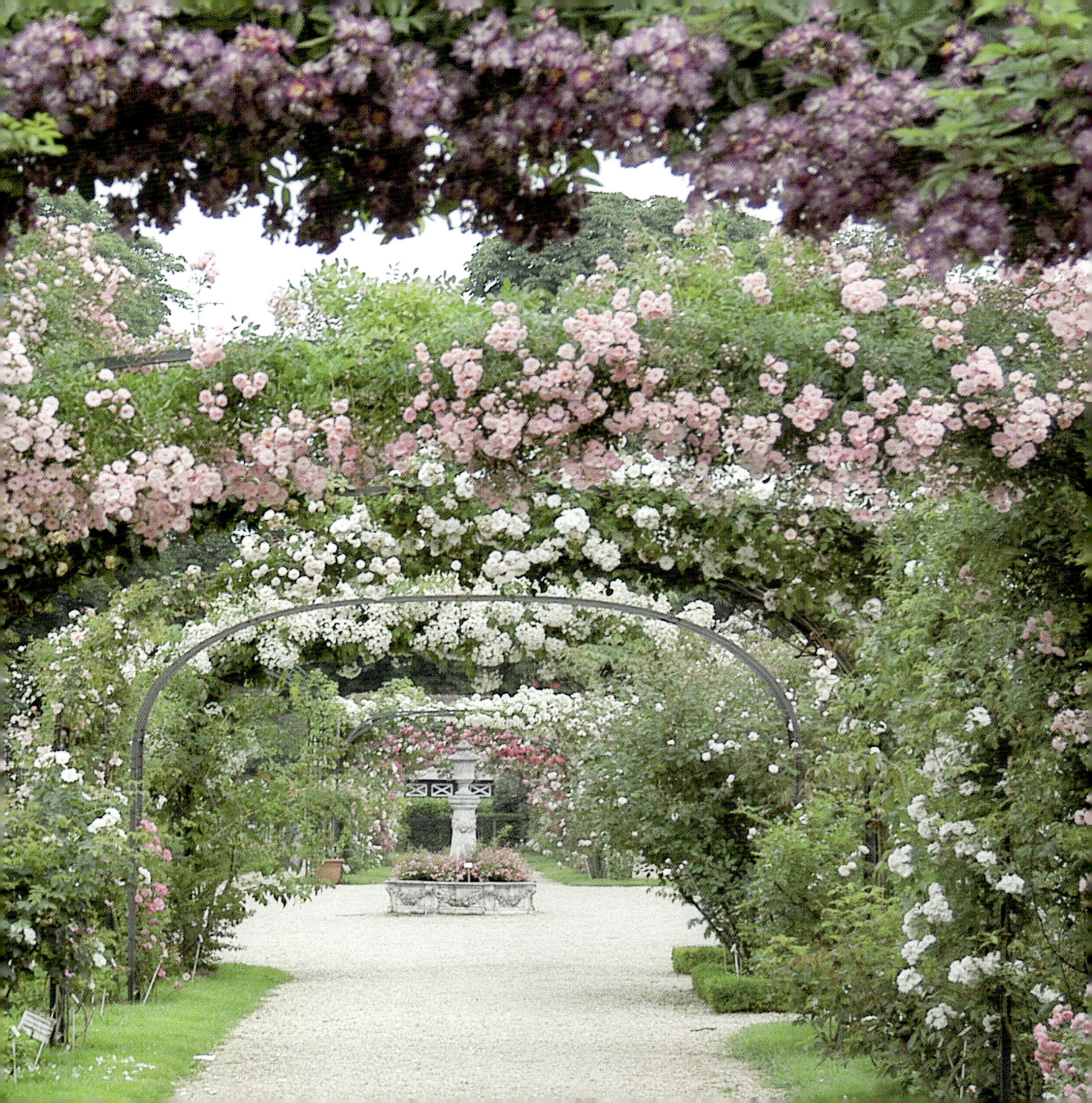

A Passion for Pink

Picking roses of the same colour is always fun. Pink is my all-time favourite colour. But lately I have been very proud of my red arrangements. Lavender shades, too, look most effective. Clusters of bright pink 'Spring Song' always attract my attention. And I have difficulty restraining myself from picking all the beautiful soft pink apple-scented blooms of 'Bonica' when they are in their prime. Often blooming with a darker pink centre, especially when the weather is cooler, this floribunda is such a good performer in our garden. No wonder it is included in the world's top ten favourite roses. Starting out with just four plants that we originally purchased seven years ago, we now have over eighty bushes in the garden that Bob has struck from cuttings. A touch of white *Gypsophila* included in an arrangement is a bonus. Many moons ago, when I worked in book publishing in New Zealand, I remember ordering a huge bunch of red roses to farewell a member of staff. When forty ruby red roses highlighted with *Gypsophila* arrived, I wished I was taking them home myself!

Bunches of the exquisite tiny soft-pink rose 'The Fairy' look adorable. They remind me of Victorian posies all tied up with bows of ribbon and lace. We now have more than fifty bushes of this rose in our garden and, although it is one of the latest to flower, it is also one

∧ 'Spring Song' is a tall shrub with gorgeous clusters of blooms. It was released in 1954.

> *Gypsophila* softens the delicate, creamy white flushed pink blooms of 'Princesse de Monaco'.

Another bed of 'Bonica' blooming prolifically.

of the longest blooming. Fairies remind me of my childhood drawings of them with their dainty, delicate wings, flitting around toadstools. I have planted a ring of 'The Fairy' to remind me of the real-life fairy ring that I once stumbled upon. Growing at the edge of a creek, it formed a perfect circle of white mushrooms. Through my eight-year-old eyes, it was easy to imagine tiny fairies flying around, sprinkling magic everywhere with their wands. I want to add some mushrooms made of stone to my fairy garden one day.

In Walter Duncan's garden we noticed a rose called 'White Fairy' but we all agreed that it was not a sport from 'The Fairy'. Its leaves and

< Shades of pink and red roses combine well in any arrangement.

> One of our 'Spring Song' bushes has lighter-coloured flowers in charming shades of pink and white.

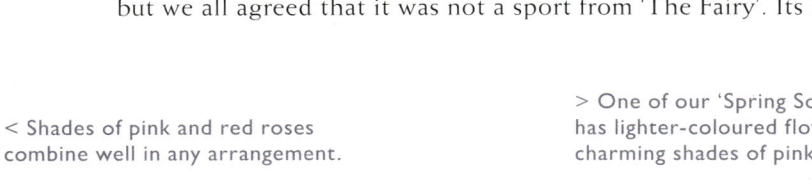

'China Doll' climbs up many structures in Paradise, including this unusual jagged stone pillar that Bob built which we named "The Bottle".

flowers were different. But in our garden a white sport has made an appearance. We are carefully observing it. As yet there is only one commercially available sport from 'The Fairy' – it is a bright pink named 'Lovely Fairy'. One of our beds has the two pink shades side by side and they look a picture. Bob and I once saw 'The Fairy' growing as a row of standards in a private garden in Paris. Their masses of weeping, frothy soft pink blooms looked so very beautiful that we decided to do the same in Paradise. Except that we will alternate the two shades of pink. As Bob believes the standards sold in nurseries are not tall enough, John Nieuwesteeg from Coldstream in Victoria is propagating them for us. Forty bushes on his own 1.5-metre-high understock.

Next winter I have three 'Super Fairy' coming. I have been told that the flowers on this rambler are the same as 'The Fairy' but there are more of them. It is hard to imagine that any more flowers could grow on our shrub bushes, so it will be interesting to see what they are like.

'China Doll' is the best climbing rose in our garden. I first saw this rose in the early 1990s at Ross Roses, south of Adelaide. My mother and I were captivated with the way huge frilly clusters of dolly pink flowers hung down right into our faces from several arches that spanned a wide walkway. It was on the same visit that we first saw 'Bonica' too – and my mother ended up buying me my first plant of it.

< L–R Charming frilly blooms of 'The Fairy'; Glorious clusters of 'China Doll'.

> The perfect apple-scented blooms of 'Bonica' are hard to surpass.

Bob and I saw once saw the human equivalent of 'China Doll'. We were shopping for Christmas decorations in China and in walked the prettiest Chinese girl, all dressed in pink – a real China doll! Our 'China Doll' walk features nine 3 m-high steel pillars smothered in cascades of pink blooms for at least nine months of the year, with an arch still to come at one end. Bob loves this rose because it has no thorns. It was first discovered growing in Queensland as a sport of the original low-growing 'China Doll' bush rose. No wonder then that it does so well in our own semi-tropical climate. Five of the bush form grow in front of our dining room window. This polyantha rose was released in America in 1946 and is supposed to grow about half a metre high. But my plants have soared up to one metre!

Just by Chance

On my daily rose walks I am constantly on the lookout for sports, which are mutations or changes. It is always exciting to discover a different shape or colour – it could mean a brand new rose. Look what happened to white 'Iceberg'. In the same private garden in Tasmania it sported three new colours – blushing pink, burgundy and brilliant pink, which have now been released as three new roses. How lucky can you get? Early this year I was trimming off spent blooms from 'Apricot Nectar'. Suddenly I stopped and stared at some unusual pink flushes on the petals of two blooms. I called Bob to investigate further. At first glance he saw nothing different, but then he noticed pink veins embellished on the blooms. And pronto we sent some budwood to John in Victoria. 'Apricot Nectar' is a vigorous grower and produces perfect cut specimens, so we are eagerly waiting to see how this new baby develops. Bob thinks it may even sport again once we get a bed of it.

Another way of obtaining new roses is to plant your own seeds. It

< I bought this statue at the Melbourne Flower Show and named her Lucy. She loves being surrounded by roses, especially 'China Doll' at her feet.

is easy to bring back seeds from overseas. Just clean them carefully and seal them in an envelope to declare to customs. Write on the envelope that they are rose seeds. Customs will either let you pass through or decide to fumigate your envelope, after which you can collect it. Near the charming village of St-Girons, close to the Pyrénées mountains in the south of France, I once plucked a few ripe seeds from a rose growing up the wall of a small Roman church. And now, the resulting rose in our garden is almost like a tall version of 'Bonica'. The sown seeds took only three months to come into flower!

Harvesting rose seeds from your own garden is fascinating. Simply pick off the red or orange hips at the end of autumn and place them in a plastic bag, then throw in a handful of dirt. Seal the bag and store in the crisper of your refrigerator until spring. Then clean the seed and sow in a seed tray. Once the seedlings are about 6 cm high, repot into individual pots. And if the flowers show promise, plant them out in your garden! But remember, only about one in every 4000 new roses make it onto the market. Since releasing their first rose in 1954, Delbard have created 257 new roses, resulting from 40,000 crossings per year!

Nearly every day I also remove dead blooms from seventy bushes of an

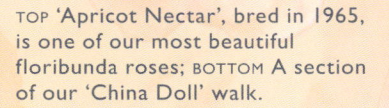

TOP 'Apricot Nectar', bred in 1965, is one of our most beautiful floribunda roses; BOTTOM A section of our 'China Doll' walk.

∧ Our exciting new sport on 'Apricot Nectar'.

167

∧ The colour of 'Lavender Dream' contrasts well with apricot, pink and white tonings.

My mother with a bunch of her rose 'Lynley's Lilac'.

exquisitely fragrant lilac, flushed pink and buff, rose that we entered in the Australian rose trial grounds at the Adelaide Botanic Gardens. We await the final judging but I have heard that its intense perfume has been well received. In the judging stakes, scent carries more points than any other characteristic. Even if it does not win an award, we will release it. It already has a name – 'Lynley's Lilac' – after my mother who has a penchant for fragrant lavender roses, especially the pretty 'Angel Face', which is one of the parents of this brand new rose.

One morning in early January I walk into the house at morning tea time with the most glorious bucket full of pink and red roses – my favourite colour combination. "Don't throw those pink roses out," says Bob. "I'll see if there's any pollen and then we can do some crossing with 'Lynley's Lilac'. You need to keep the flowers inside so that the bees don't get to the pollen." What fun I immediately have thinking of

< Our own new rose 'Lynley's Lilac' is a chance seedling from 'Angel Face'.

all the crosses I would like to carry out. And over the next month we pollinate about 250 flowers with all sorts of combinations. Bob often lies awake at night in bed thinking about the possible results of his crosses, not just of roses – and now so do I!

It's an easy process once you get the hang of it. First, choose the flower you are going to use the pollen from. Then pluck its petals and the pollen will ripen to a texture like talcum powder. Gently dust this pollen, using the flower itself, onto the stigma you have emasculated by cutting off all its stamens. Small scissors can be used to effectively carry out this job. When the pollen touches the stigma, you should see it instantly darken in colour. Cover the seed with a paper bag to keep out unwanted bees. After a few days the pollen grains should have germinated and fertilised the ovaries. Then harvest in autumn and plant

> (following pages) Nothing can surpass the innate beauty of rose buds.

v This bed, dominated by eleven 'Apricot Nectar', five 'Iceberg' and five 'Lavender Dream', makes a lovely entrance to the garden at the top of our driveway.

^ 'Lovely Fairy' makes a real show in our garden with its masses of bright pink flowers, which bloom for many months.

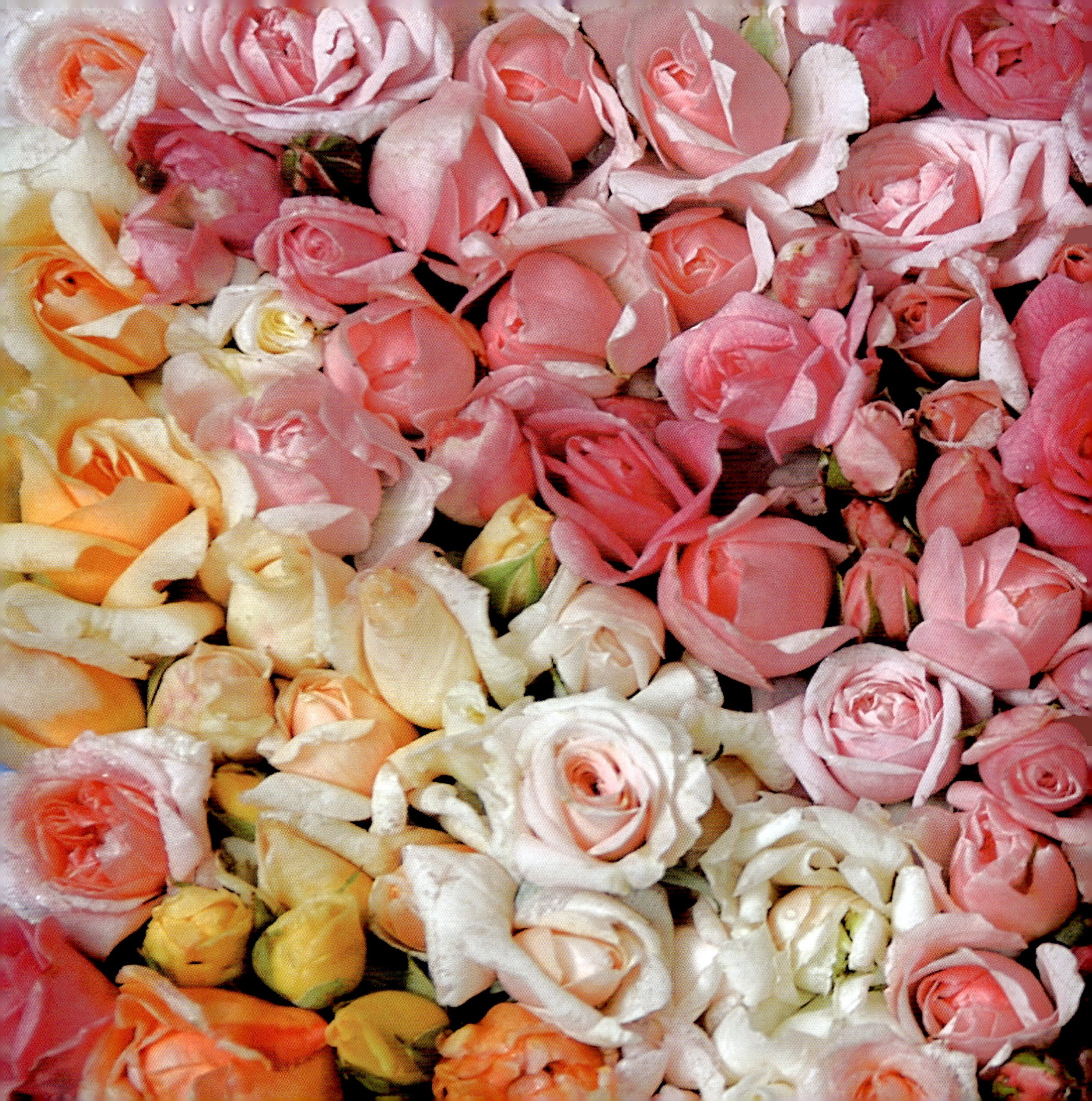

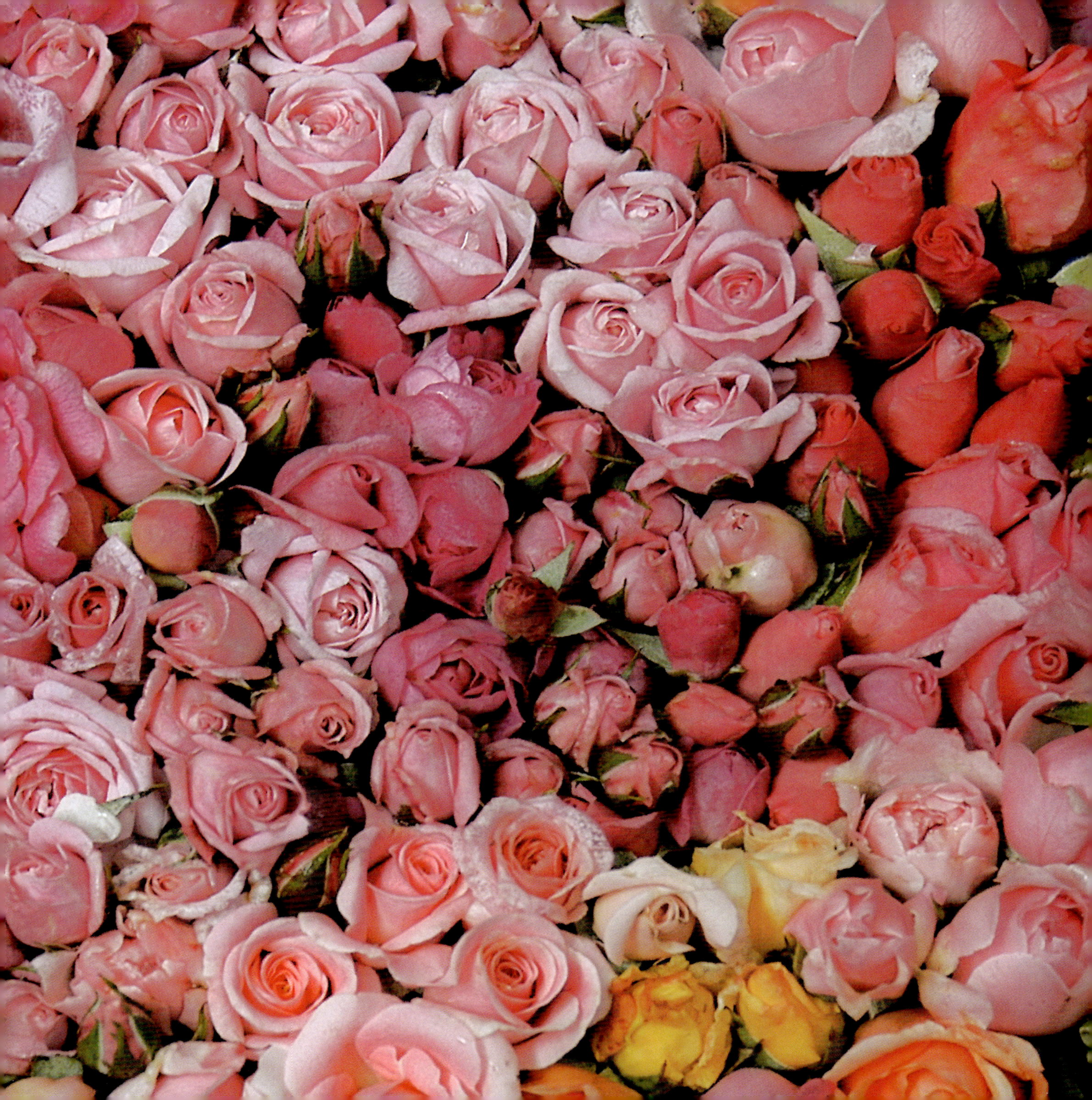

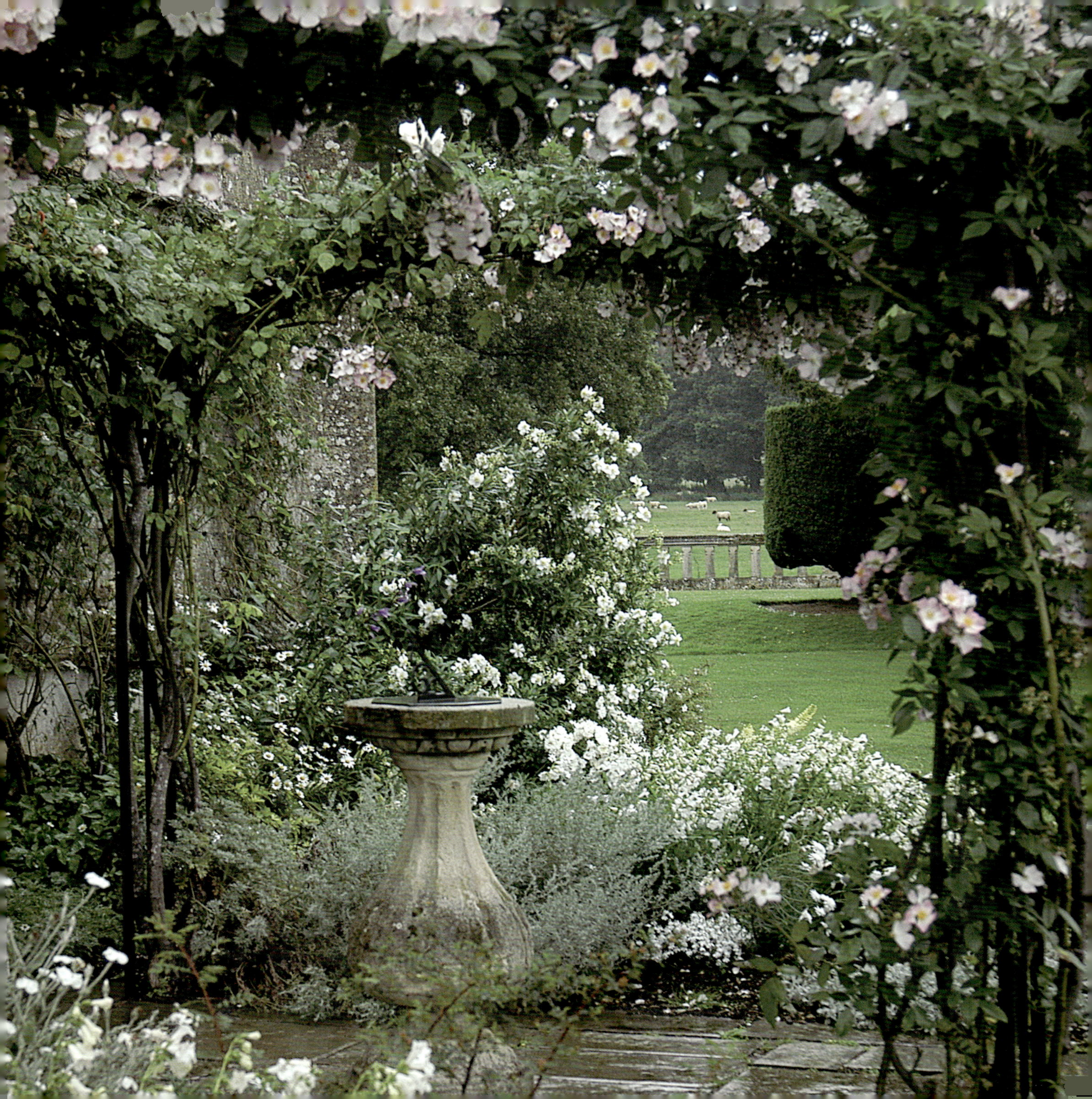

out in spring as previously described (see page 167).

Bob has often been asked how to take rose cuttings. His advice is very simple. Midsummer is the best time, when the wood is semi-hard. Find a stem or heel, which you can even snap off with your fingers. Cut off the flowers and trim back to one or two leaves. Either dip it in hormone powder or honey and then plant it in a pot in a mixture of peat and sand. Cover the pot with a plastic bag and place it in a shaded position; within six weeks roots and shoots will appear, with flowers soon after.

His other method is to take hardwood cuttings while pruning in winter. Just below a node, cut off a piece about 300 mm long that includes two or three nodes or buds. Wrap it in a slightly damp paper towel, seal in a plastic bag and place in the refrigerator. After one month callus tissue (like a scab) will have formed at the base of the cutting. Around the end of August, before spring, either plant it in a pot with one or two nodes protruding from the soil or, using a stick, simply poke a hole in the ground where you want it to grow. Nine times out of ten, it will grow into a healthy plant that will flower within a few months.

< Called the "Queen's Garden", this rose garden is in the grounds of Sudeley Castle in England's Cotswold Hills. Henry VIII's sixth wife, Catherine Parr, who once owned this castle, is buried here.

∧ This bed of Grafton Pink was cut back and flowered again only four weeks later! (see p. 157)

Some of my Garden Favourites*

'Ashram' – Hybrid tea, Tanmarsa, 2006, striking large old gold blooms

'Abraham Darby' – Shrub, David Austin, England, 1985, gorgeous pink peach and apricot blends in this fragrant cup-shaped rose

'Baroque' – Ground cover, Harkness, England, 1995, semi-double magenta blooms

'Belle Story' – Shrub, David Austin, England, 1984, delicate and lovely pale pinky apricot cup-shaped flowers with gold stamens; fragrant

'Bloomfield Abundance' – Floribunda, USA, 1941, variation of 'Cécile Brunner' but grows much taller – makes lovely sprays for picking

'Bordure Magenta' – Floribunda, Delbard, France, 1994, attractive bright pink clusters

'Brass Band' – Floribunda, USA, 1993, profuse bloomer, clusters of attractive melon, orange and yellow ruffled flowers

'Charles de Gaulle' – Hybrid tea, Meilland, 1974 – one of my most fragrant formal lavender roses

'Chartreuse de Parme' – Shrub, Delbard, France, 1996, simply stunning regal purple colour with fragrance to match – won awards in Europe for most fragrant rose

'Chicago Peace' Hybrid tea, USA, 1962, this sport of 'Peace' has exquisite pink, yellow and apricot shades but unfortunately dislikes our humid climate – blooms with huge flowers in drier climate of Adelaide

'Crépuscule' – Noisette, Dubreuil, France, 1904, small butterscotch-coloured flowers that blend well with other colours – useful contrast in the garden, especially with pinks

'Elina' – Hybrid tea, Dickson, Ireland, 1984, tall growing; large elegant lemon flowers with lots of blooms that repeat well

'Europeana' – Climbing floribunda, 1987, clusters of crimson velvet fragrant blooms with attractive glossy foliage – it is a sport of the original 'Europeana' floribunda released by De Ruiter in Belgium in 1963

'Fiona's Wish' – Hybrid tea, Meilland, 1996, outstanding bloom with cherry red touched gold petals – wonderful in mixed rose arrangements, it was released in Europe under the name of 'Meizuzes'

'Fisherman's Friend' – Shrub, David Austin, England, 1988, large deep ruby/purple double, cupped blooms with intense damask fragrance – very prickly but unforgettable

'François Juranville' – Wichurana rambler, Barbier, France, 1906, pink flushed apricot and lemon fragrant blooms make a wonderful early show; some repeats

---

* Favourites are categorised by type of rose, breeder and/or country of origin where known, and date of release.

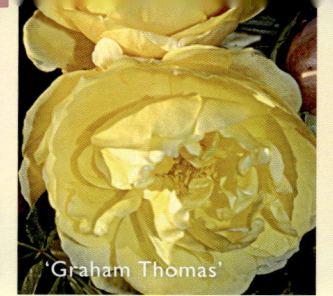

'Belle Story' 'Le Vésuve' 'Fiona's Wish' 'Graham Thomas' 'Olde Fragrance'

'Gertrude Jekyll' – Shrub, David Austin, England, 1986, superb fragrance; lovely, almost luminescent pink, used in David Austin's breeding programme for fragrance

'Golden Fairytale' – Hybrid tea, Korquelda, 2006, lovely clusters of quartered scented mid-yellow flowers

'Graham Thomas' – Shrub, David Austin, England, 1983, the biggest and best yellow in the Austin collection for us – masses of cupped golden yellow flowers, perfect for picking

'Grand Siècle' – Hybrid tea, Delbard, France, 1986, very large pale pink blooms

'Granada' – Hybrid tea, USA, 1963, gaily coloured, attractive and unusual, apricot yellow and pink shades

'Home and Garden' – Floribunda, Korgrasotra, 2003, clusters of romantic pink; low-growing, makes a very pretty specimen plant

> Any rose arrangement adds a touch of romance.

'Kardinal' – Hybrid tea, Kordes, Germany, 1985, bright red classic-shaped blooms that repeat well and last a long time as cut flowers

'Lavender Mist' – Large-flowered climber, USA, 1981, an elegant mauve, long-lasting cut flower specimen, good tall grower

'Le Vésuve' – China rose, Laffay, France, 1825, lovely nostalgic pink blooms

'Manita' – Large-flowered climber, Kordes, Germany, 1996, very vigorous climber with masses of semi-double mid pink ruffled blooms for a spectacular display

'Mary Rose' – Shrub, David Austin, England, 1983, intense scent, silky lavender-pink petals, low grower, lovely garden specimen

'Molineux' – Shrub, David Austin, England, 1994, attractive lemon with darker yellow centre, rosette-shaped flower, inner petals sometimes flushed pale apricot

'Monsieur Tillier' – Tea rose, Bernaix, France, 1891, tall-

∧ The early French rose 'François Juranville' never fails to make a spectacular old-fashioned first flush.

growing; pink flushed coral blooms for most of the year

'My Choice' – Hybrid tea, Le Grice, England, 1958, pink flushed yellow fragrant blooms

'Nana Mouskouri' – Floribunda, Ireland, 1975, creamy white clusters, prolific bloomer – provides good contrast to other colours, especially pinks and apricots

'Olde Fragrance' – Hybrid tea, Germany, 1986, lives up to its name – magnificent purple/pink blooms, very fragrant – tall grower

'Pat Austin' – Shrub, David Austin, England, 1997, a bright coppery orange that highlights other colours

'Perfume Delight' – Hybrid tea, USA, 1973, deep pink blooms with long stems that last well as cut flowers; strong grower with intense damask scent

'Portrait' – Hybrid tea, USA, 1971, very pretty double pale to mid-pink fragrant blooms – called 'Stéphanie de Monaco' in Europe

'Red Pierre' – Large-flowered climber, France, a pillar rose with attractive old-fashioned quartered crimson flowers

'Renae' – Climbing floribunda, USA, 1954, one of Bob's favourites as it has no thorns; clusters of pretty, soft pink blooms over a very long period

'Rhapsody in Blue' – Shrub, England, 1999, dark mauve/purple unusual-coloured clusters of flowers – good contrast with hot pink

'Roundelay' – Grandiflora, USA, 1954, attractive red that produces masses of flowers over a very long period – excellent cut flower specimen

'Savoy Hotel' – Hybrid tea, Harkness, England, 1987, large double pale pink, extremely elegant blooms often with darker pink centre, perfect for cutting and arranging

'Sympathie' – Kordesii hybrid, Kordes, Germany, 1964, wonderful, very fragrant dark

∧ 'Pat Austin' is a lovely, unusual burnt coppery colour that looks stunning in mixed beds.

∧ 'Rhapsody in Blue' was winner of the Rose of the Year award in England in 2003. Even though it is not a true blue, there are few similar roses.

'Renae' makes a lovely display in the garden.

velvet red flowers, sweet fragrance, grows vigorously for us as a climber
'Swan' – Shrub, David Austin, England, 1987, attractive creamy white blooms borne in clusters, good cut flower that lasts well
'Teasing Georgia' – Shrub, David Austin, England, 1998, pale lemon, grows superbly and continues to bloom with masses of flowers over a very long period – one of our best Austins – need to keep its long arching branches trimmed in our climate
'Tess of the D'Urbervilles' – Shrub, David Austin, England, 1998, terribly prickly but strikingly attractive cerise bud and flower; blooms profusely
'The Children's Rose' – Hybrid tea, Meilland, France, 1993, very tall, vigorous grower with delectable pale pink blooms and an intense damask fragrance; released as 'Frédéric Mistral' in Europe

'Traviata' – Hybrid tea, Meilland, France, 1998, lots of impressive dark red blooms, tall strong grower, but many nasty prickles

'Violina' – Hybrid tea, Tantau, Germany, 1997, extremely shapely long pointy buds open to impressive large mid-pink flowers

'Valencia' – Hybrid tea, Kordes, Germany, 1989, elegant old-gold apricot colour with strong fragrance, long stems perfect for cutting and lasts well

'Winchester Cathedral' – Shrub, David Austin, England, 1992, lovely ruffled pristine white sport of 'Mary Rose'

∧ Somehow the luscious creamy lemon blooms of the 'Swan' remind me of those beautiful white birds from the Northern Hemisphere.

∧ 'Teasing Georgia' is another of our best yellows that blooms on and on.

∧ 'Winchester Cathedral' is a lovely ruffled pure white with an intense scent.

In the Name of a Rose

This moss rose, named 'Celina' dates back to 1855.

Names of roses fascinate me. Amongst the walled rose garden at Hever Castle in Surrey, England is a wonderful dark red rose. The curiously named 'Deep Secret' now grows in our garden and its rich velvety petals remind me of the tragic Anne Boleyn, for it was at Hever Castle that she spent some of her childhood years. On one of our visits to this stately castle, magnificent rose arrangements adorned all rooms open to the public. I remember contemplating the display in the tiny bedroom where Anne used to sleep and wondering what her favourite colours would have been. Although roses in her day were mainly red, white and pink.

David Austin roses have come to be known as the 'English Roses'. No wonder, the names he has chosen are so evocative of that country: 'Warwick Castle', 'Jude the Obscure', 'William Shakespeare' and even 'English Garden' to name but a few. When we visited his nursery and display garden in Shropshire, I was delighted to watch how the spent blooms were left on the ground after dead-heading. With so many roses to look after, it was the sensible thing to do – a habit I have adopted here in Paradise! As I finished photographing yet another rose, Bob suddenly said "David Austin just walked past you." And yes, the man himself had just opened the gate from his house adjoining the garden. But I was too busy concentrating on his roses!

'Squatter's Dream' is another rose that conjures up nostalgic images for me. Bred by Australia's most famous rose breeder, Alister Clark, in 1923, it has clusters of yellow-buff single blooms with golden stamens. It takes me back to my research on colonial Australia when I was writing my doctoral thesis at the University of Sydney. My subject was the life of Colonial Secretary Alexander Macleay of Elizabeth Bay House, who had a variety of interests, including farming. Alister Clark's father, Walter, managed several of Alexander's extensive rural properties in the 1840s.

In 1853 Walter built the lovely homestead and garden called Glenara, which is still there today adjacent to Melbourne's Tullamarine Airport. Alexander Macleay, who died in 1848, was a great lover of roses and had even brought several plants out with him from England when he arrived in Sydney in 1826. Although Alister did not commence his rose breeding at Glenara until 1912, it is tempting to think that he may have used cuttings from some of Alexander's roses. After all, Alexander's glorious 22-hectare garden in Sydney at Elizabeth Bay was deemed one of the finest in the colony in the 1830s.

Strangely, the rose called 'Paradise' was my favourite when I lived in my 1870s whaler's cottage at North Sydney in the early 1990s. Its finely pointed lavender bud opens to reveal lilac petals tinged with magenta, finally fading to rose magenta shades. It's like having three roses in one. How apt that I planted it right by my front gate – although when I ended up living in Paradise I found out that Bob had never heard of this rose!

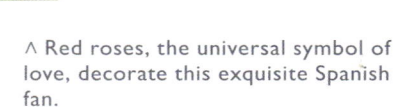

∧ Red roses, the universal symbol of love, decorate this exquisite Spanish fan.

∧ Bob reading and relaxing in the evening, surrounded by our animal children.

< Trudy loves watching the lizards on this rock near our back door.

A Life of Roses

When we first visited David Ruston's rose garden in Renmark some years ago, it was winter. I finally saw it in all its glory last October on our way to Adelaide. I recalled how delighted David was to catch up with Bob again on our first visit. They had travelled together with a group of rose enthusiasts about thirty years before to attend a rose festival in America. And how thrilled I was to have the opportunity to discuss roses with such a famous expert. "Roses are easy to arrange – they lend themselves to it," he told me. But not everyone has the skill, flair and knowledge that he has – down to every detail and the history of each rose that he uses.

Our visit coincided with the Renmark Rose Festival. We visited several lovely local gardens, but the real highlight for me was the display in the Renmark Institute, where some of the arrangements had been done by David Ruston. This display, locally organised, impressed me so much. I liked the nostalgic mix of history and roses – but best of all were the roses. The hall was laid out in five sections, each one representing an important occasion in the life of a fictitious girl, with an overall theme of "Life in a Country Garden". In fact her character was an amalgamation of real characters who had lived in a local historic house called "Chowilla". The scenes moved from her marriage in 1891, aged twenty, to include a child's christening, a harvest thanksgiving festival,

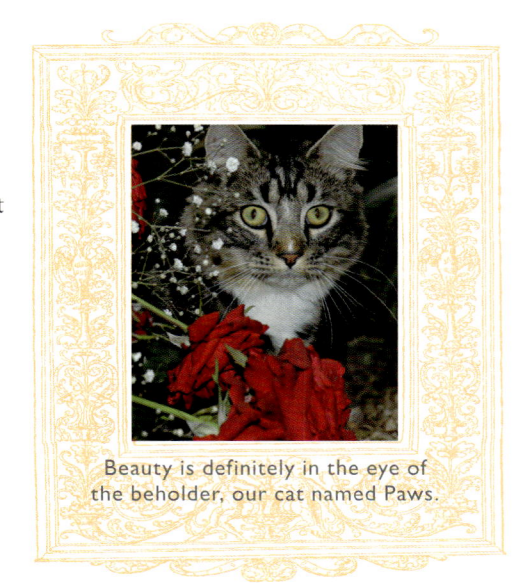

∧ One of David Ruston's magnificent arrangements in the Renmark Institute during their Rose Festival.

< This gallica rose 'Versicolor' ('Rosa Mundi') has been enjoyed by gardeners for hundreds of years.

Beauty is definitely in the eye of the beholder, our cat named Paws.

Christmas, a Melbourne Cup horse race party and a formal dinner party to celebrate a golden wedding anniversary. Mannequins in period costume brought everything to life and the backdrop on the stage was a huge painting of the old house. There was even a reproduction tombstone with names and dates. And everywhere there were stunning arrangements of colour-coordinated roses. Particularly exquisite were the pink and white posies, using 'Bonica' and 'Iceberg', that decked the church pews set out for the wedding. I was totally enraptured.

Roses have become such big business in our enterprising world of today. Since patents were introduced in the 1950s, more new rose varieties have exploded onto the international market than ever before. Now there are so many new roses, it is hard to keep up with them all. At lunch today Bob commented, "You have quite a nice floribunda seedling out; you should bring it down to plant in the garden." I had seen this one a few days ago – it was my favourite mid-pink colour. "I want to go about this scientifically, so could you please count the number of petals on it and 'Bonica'?" I ask. The small cluster of flowers reminds me so much of 'Bonica'. "Forty-six on the new one and twenty-four on 'Bonica'," replies Bob. "Could be alright, but what about that black spot?" he continues. "But it has no thorns!" I point out. "Could be interesting," he finally agrees.

I am convinced that a true blue-coloured rose is not that far away either. But one characteristic still remains constant throughout the world. Place a rose in front of most people and they will automatically want to smell it. This magnetic charm of the rose is what continues to attract and captivate me. Give me a bucket of rose blooms any day and I will be content.

∧ A sundial adorned with 'Bonica' and 'Simply Magic', with highlights of Geraldton wax, looked so very pretty amongst the setting for the Melbourne Cup celebrations in the Renmark Institute.

This self-sown *Dahlia* veritably glows in the garden.

Colour Parade

"the love of gardening is a seed that once sown never dies" GERTRUDE JEKYLL

Red, White and Blue

When I was commissioning gardening books, I was once asked to compile a list of titles for future gardening books. After all, that's what commissioning editors were supposed to do – come up with creative ideas! At that time white gardens were in favour, so I included colour themes in the list. Just like the clothing industry, gardening follows fashion as well. Perhaps the late Christopher Lloyd could be described as one of the gardening world's fashion icons. The famous garden surrounding his manor house in England, called "Great Dixter", set many new trends. When I visited this East Sussex splendour for the first time, with Bob, we admired a bed of orange marigolds mixed with purple *Celosia*. Not a colour scheme that I would have chosen, but it was certainly eye-catching and different. Bob was only interested in the garden, but I joined a tour of the house. As our group stood in the Great Hall on the ground floor, I observed a door opening at one end and a diminutive man quietly walking away behind us. Was this the great man, I wondered? After the introductory talk ended, we entered the room that had just been evacuated. It turned out to be Christopher Lloyd's study, where he wrote his masterpieces! I will never forget my close encounter!

∧ Richly coloured *Pelargonium* flowers are like precious jewels scattered throughout the garden.

∧ Larkspur soften any landscape with their glorious shades, especially this purple flower edged with lavender blue.

> Pelargoniums climb up our steel structures for a continuous show of stunning colour.

Our bed of dainty, self-sown *Linaria*.

Orange *Cosmos* flowers profusely in front of our monkey colony.

Sow Your Own

Our annuals are mostly either self-sown, or grown from seed that we collected the previous year and raised as seedlings. People always comment on and admire the *Linaria* bed. "But you can't buy seeds of it anymore," complained one visitor recently. In actual fact, it is readily available in seed packets at nurseries – but only occasionally in punnets. Other seeds that come up of their own accord in our garden are lupins, which Bob loves, and larkspur. Also columbines (*Aquilegia*), often called "grannies bonnets", whose spiky, fairy-like petals in their delicate pastel shades are so old-fashioned looking, and all of our daisies, which can always be relied on to make a wonderful display. Our stock and *Primula* beds are a combination of self-sown varieties and seedlings. Annual plantings of our seedlings, for spring colour, are best done before the end of February to encourage some growth in the warm late autumn weather before winter begins. Pansies and violas will then flower from April right through until Christmas.

> Rows of hollyhocks have often been seen in Paradise.

This bed of *Arctotis* (African daisy) is constantly in flower for many months of the year.

> Spreading over one of our stone walls, this self-sown variegated *Petunia* captured everyone's attention.

Dogs and self-sown seeds are not always the best combination. One day we noticed that Trudy could hardly walk. When we investigated further, we discovered that her paws were full of the burr-like seeds of forget-me-nots – no wonder she was almost crippled! And they are a nightmare to remove. These days Bob has banned forget-me-nots from the garden for that reason, although I do miss their lovely blue flowers. *Bidens* seeds are Jessee's favourite. Somehow she always manages to come back from below the chook house with them sticking out all over her fur – and, yet again, they have to be patiently removed, one by one!

When Bob was a wee lad, living at Tascott on the Central Coast of New South Wales, he looked forward to his spring and summer holidays. At those times, he always travelled to Sydney by train, not to enjoy the fantastic waterways which he passed on the way, but to see the wonderful beds of annuals on display at the different railway stations. Especially outside Chatswood station, where there was a kaleidoscope of colour. In spring, stock, pansies, *Cineraria* and, occasionally, the flamboyant *Schizanthus* took his fancy. And each summer, *Phlox*, *Petunia*, bright mixed colour beds of *Portulaca*, *Zinnia*, bright red and some yellow *Celosia*, and the colourful yellow and scarlet *Amaranthus* variety (known as Joseph's coat of many colours) caught his eye. Even though he already had his own garden at that young age, he was determined to always have beds of massed colour wherever he made a garden in the future.

A Wee Lad and a Wee Lassie

< Trudy, forever the vigilant gardener, amongst miniature snapdragons.

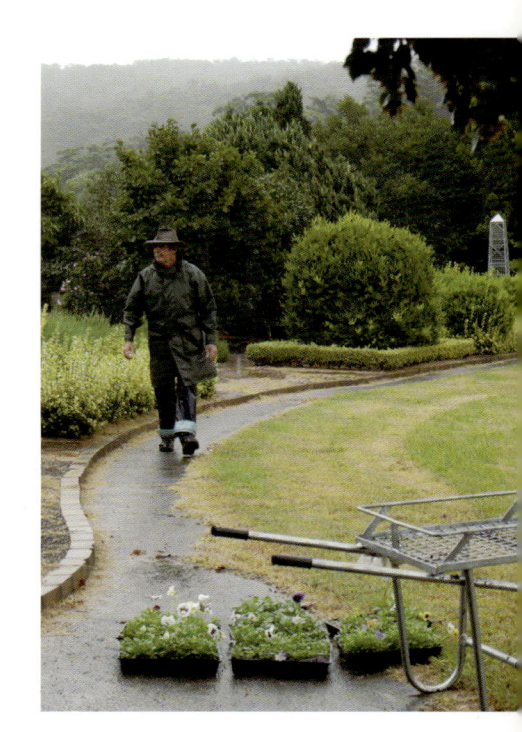

> Come rain or shine, the planting must go on.

∨ Although they were only artificial flowers, I just loved this posy when I was a five-year-old debutante.

Bob is very keen on *Alstromeria*, which have a bed of their own.

For me, as a wee lassie, the sweet smelling *Alyssum* was always a favourite. How many hours I spent, during my years at primary school, painstakingly arranging tiny *Alyssum* and *Lantana* flowers – and many others, including single petals – in the saucers of wet sand that we were given to make our own floral carpet. Curiously, Bob also recalls making these in his childhood – except that in his case they were called "decorated saucers". It was great fun but extraordinarily time-consuming. Although the tiny blue flowers of the *Plumbago* were sticky to work with, and did not last very long, they looked ever so pretty. Violets were another popular choice for these arrangements, as were violas and pansies, especially the ones with appealing little faces. Even now they are still our favourites in the garden. And this form of art with flowers continues to this day – our local Mangrove Mountain Country Fair has a children's competition each year for the best "decorated saucer in wet sand".

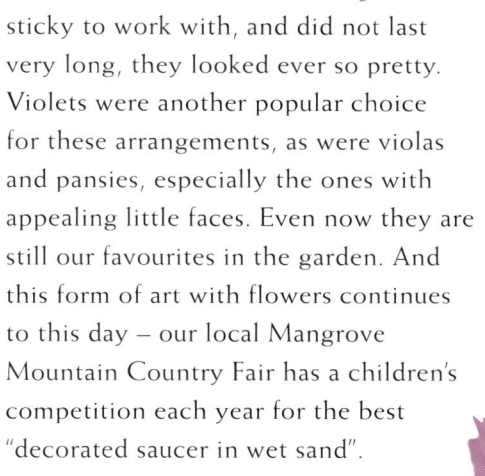

∧ *Cosmos* comes up of its own accord everywhere, but it is such a lovely addition to the garden that it is never removed.

Trudy, and a very young Jessee, posing in front of sweet-smelling lavender *Alyssum*.

> This shade of *Cosmos* looks the most appealing in our garden setting.

< *Alstromeria* is well worth growing because the blooms last so long after picking.

Massed beds of yellow and white violas make a good contrast with the gold of our boxed hedges and tall white stock in the background.

A Patch of Phlox

Whenever I pick a small bunch of *Phlox* to arrange in the house, I am charmed by their simple beauty. Their tiny flowers, in the prettiest shades, have always delighted me. One year we planted out some seed we had sent away for from an English catalogue. The flowers were in pastel shades of mostly apricot, pink and cream and, much to my surprise, they were the best we had ever grown. We have vases for all sorts of flowers and whenever Bob spots another that he likes, he immediately thinks about what flowers would look good in it.

∧ Petunias flower for such a long time. There is even a variety named 'Colour Parade' which is a mix of vivid clear colours.

> Snapdragons, such as this beauty, and foxgloves, appear again year after year.

> "Pansies for thoughts" must have been constantly in the mind of Bette Lorraine Quick when she designed and embroidered this piano stool for her daughter, Diane.

One flower is ubiquitous in Paradise. So much so that you would think it was native to this area. Commonly known as Lady's Slipper, because of the shape of its small bright yellow flowers, it has spread everywhere like a weed. Bob brought the seed back from England but says he has seen it growing in the wild in Mexico, under forests of a weeping pine called *Pinus patula*. It is called *Calceolaria fothergillii*. Although it is not one of my favourites, it is amazing how many people admire it and want to know what it is. I always reply, "Please pull some out and take them home – you will be doing me a favour."

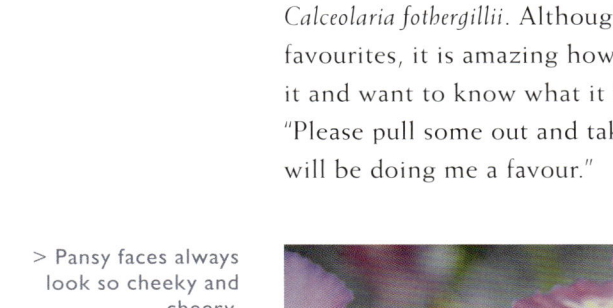

> Pansy faces always look so cheeky and cheery.

< My Nanna loved delicate flowers, especially violets and the frilly lacy petals of *Scabiosa*.

> This has always been my favourite photograph of my Nanna, Vida Muriel Stanton Hamlyn. I am sure it is because of the flowery setting. On 23 November 1910 she married Albert William Cornish, in the small Adelaide Hills township of Gumeracha.

"We do not all want to float endlessly among silvers, greys and tender pinks in the gentle nicotiana-laden ambient of a summer's gloaming. Some prefer a bright, brash midday glare with plenty of stuffing" CHRISTOPHER LLOYD

> Massed blooms of azaleas, set amongst the scrub in the Blue Mountains Rhododendron Garden at Blackheath, are truly inspirational.

< The "touch of blue" principle perfects this arrangement of dahlias and roses.

A Touch of Blue

Somehow a touch of blue works in every garden. The bright blue flowers that sprout on the clumping foliage of *Tradescantia* and also come in shades of lavender, pink, purple and white, constantly attract attention and create bright spots throughout the year. And the lovely blue perennial aster, growing from seed that Bob collected in China, is delightful both in the garden and in mixed floral arrangements inside the house. In summer, the various blues of *Lobelia* add a wonderful contrast; and another of Bob's favourite blues is *Vinca*, which he likes to use as a groundcover, especially under roses. But I still have to do the hand-weeding in those areas! In my opinion the mat-forming purple *Verbena* is hard to beat, because it displays so many pretty bright purple blooms over such a long period.

> *Lobelia* is one of the best annuals for adding a touch of blue.

My Mystical Flower Lady

In our bedroom there is a small porcelain figurine. I call her my flower lady. She has the appearance of Meissen china, and when I first saw her in 1992, she sat on top of a magnificent 2-metre-high mahogany chest of drawers in the antique market at Buenos Aires, Argentina. I felt an instant attraction, but sadly walked away. She was quite expensive, and I had spotted an antique fan and several other things that I also wanted to buy. Yet I felt compelled to look at her again, not once but several

∨ My porcelain "flower lady" lingers among the dainty *Phlox* blooms.

< Bob believes that all flower colours go well together, as shown in this cottage garden belonging to Bill and Shirley Thomas at Victor Harbour. I remember this garden very well, because Bill's parents, Hilda and Arthur Thomas, were best friends with my grandparents who lived just across the road.

∧ A huge boulder of sandstone is the perfect backdrop for these attractive *Verbena*, which flowered month after month.

times, walking back and forward from one end of the market to the other where she was on sale. Finally I just knew that I had to buy her. She was to be mine, although I had no idea why.

She wears a magnificent 18th century costume in pink, with a pattern of red roses. Her dress is edged in blue, with a white underskirt. Of special interest for a flower lover is the fact that she carries a gilt basket in each hand, filled with pale pink, blue and lemon flowers. There is a German mark on the bottom and I have often contemplated the stories that my flower lady could relay if only she could talk. I feel sure that she left Germany after World War II – and who knows what family she belonged to there. Maybe it was even a Nazi who originally owned her. I will never know; but, without a doubt, she has ended up in the right home amongst our thousands of flowers.

What fun we have creeping towards our friend, who stares back at us.

On Bunny Hill

A Giant Rat?

We're on our evening walk to Bunny Hill with Mum and Dad when suddenly we dogs freeze. We are near the end of the lake and dusk is falling. Ears pricked, we listen hard while our hearts go faster than ever. What is that scent in the air? Is our friend the wobbly wallaby having its grass supper tonight? What fun!

We creep along a bit further, crouched low so it can't see us, and stop again in our tracks. At last we reach the top of the slope and look down. Sometimes we just hear "bong bong" as our friend lopes off back into the scrub. But sometimes we come face to face with this funny furry animal. It's so exciting! We stare at it – hard – and it stares right back at us. It feels like this goes on forever, but it's probably only for a few seconds – and then we make our move. We dogs fly off, but our wallaby somehow always manages to get away. I think this is because it has longer legs than us. It looks a bit like a giant grey rat.

^ I'm always on the alert for Mum to tell her what I have found.

> We dogs thought these tortoises were pretty interesting, especially when they started to move.

Bunny Hill

We're making our way up to Bunny Hill, which is one of our favourite places here in Paradise. It's just across the lake from the house, but you have to go on a lovely long walk to get to it. Dad wants to make it into an island one day, so that we dogs and the rest of the family can be buried there in a family vault, which he also plans to build. He has already made another memorial for our sisters near the entrance to the garden. They lived here a long time ago and Dad has quite rightly inscribed their memorial "To a man's best friend".

Bunnies scamper around us in all directions on Bunny Hill. Dad and Mum think we can't see them, but we just take our time. There are so many to enjoy. And finally they all disappear and run off to their beds inside Bunny Hill. The truth is, we can't really be bothered with the bunnies. It's the hares we prefer – we streak after them like greyhounds when we spot them.

Bunny Hill is so pretty. It's where the pinecones come from for our cosy winter fires. Lately the gum trees there have been shedding their bark; in the evening light, they look like magnificent monsters.

About a year ago, after a whole week of really heavy rain, we found a charming little waterfall underneath the bridge at the end of the lake. We played in the water for a while, splashing and swimming around, and then we saw them – six really weird-looking striped and patterned rocks. Or were they? As we watched, they slowly took off along the lawn! Four little legs appeared on each one and then a little head poked out one end. At first we were a bit scared; we had never seen anything like this before. But Mum and Dad didn't seem to mind. They were tortoises. Dad picked them up and turned them over one by one, then handed the biggest one to Mum. She seemed a bit nervous about touching it at first.

Other animals that live in Bunny Hill are wombats. They look like

∧ Dad sometimes affectionately calls me wombat and I suppose I do look a little bit like the real thing.

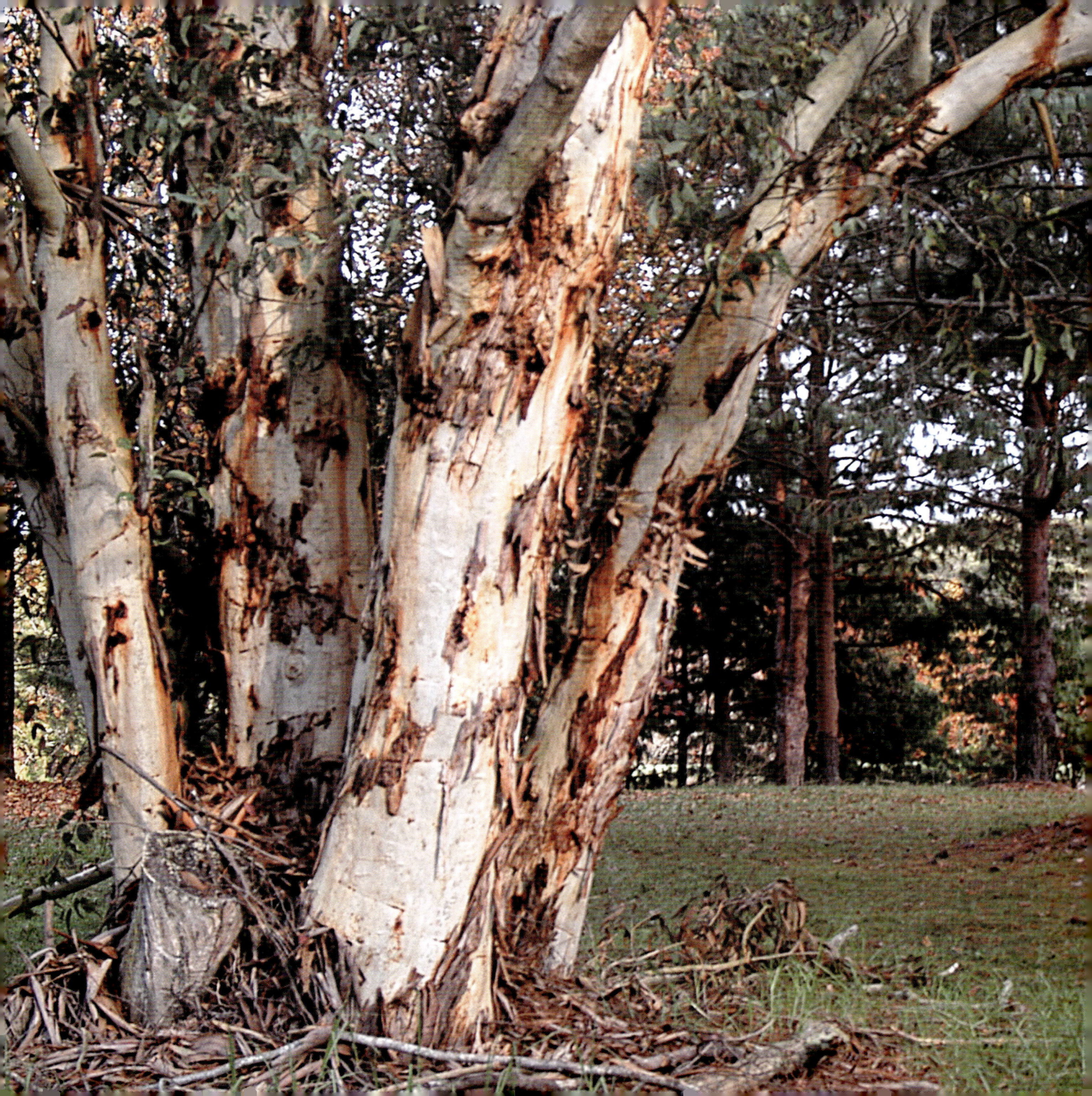

The gum trees on Bunny Hill, such as this *Eucalyptus haemastoma* (scribbly gum), are magnificent.

∧ Our diamond python looks really malevolent, even though it isn't poisonous.

Welcome to our Garden!

small bears. They're bigger than I am and have pretty strong front feet, so Jessee and I keep out of their way as much as possible. They've built lots and lots of houses inside this hill, all with interconnecting tunnels. I'm lucky because I can go exploring in them – Jessee is too big to fit in. Sometimes I think I might get stuck, but I always manage to get out. Dad thinks I might catch "wombat mange", but I'm not afraid. I'm a tough little dog. And I only go in when I know no-one's at home.

We love all the different animals in our garden. We're never bored. Why, just the other day, when a film crew arrived, our pet diamond python put on a great show. It's nearly 3 metres long and usually lives in the rafters above the staff lunchroom. But this day it climbed right to the top of a dwarf pine tree. You simply could not miss it. We dogs like sniffing around underneath this tree, because it's pretty private inside there under the bushy branches. Well, did it create a scene! The presenter was quite scared, but brave Mum took lots of photos, standing only a couple of feet away from it. Dad told her afterwards that it could have sprung out and nipped her – although it is not poisonous.

Another animal we're particularly fond of is the lyrebird. They keep us pretty busy as they're so hard to track down. Once we did manage to bail one up in a tree and keep it there for about an hour. That was a special day! They're a funny bird because they copy sounds – they even mimic Mum calling "Hoy!" to Dad when she wants to find him around the garden. And they mimic other animals too, although I haven't yet heard them bark.

There are some really big things, called goannas, that frighten us if we get too close. Even though I'm the smaller dog, I'm braver than Jessee; she's sometimes a bit timid. She always wants me to go and check things out first. We don't mind the little geckos, whose tails we can bite off in an instant and they still keep wriggling, nor most of the other lizards, but the big goannas are another thing. They have enormous front legs and I think, given a chance, they could easily tear us dogs apart. So, although we try to scare them by barking really loudly, we keep our distance.

Just the other day, we saw the strangest thing in Paradise. When Mum was cooking dinner, Dad came in and said "Turn the dinner off and come with me." So off we all trotted down to the

^ All sorts of mushrooms grow on Bunny Hill, but nobody ever eats them because they are bad for you.

∧ Dad, Jessee and I were fascinated by this enormous eel. It was the first one I had seen in Paradise, and it was so slippery, with funny little fins.

end of the lake, with Dad carrying a hoe in one hand and a stick in the other. In the overflow pool at the end of the lake, Dad fished out the most peculiar thing. It was like a thick black–blue shiny snake, but it had two small fins and made a funny little grunt as it lay on the ground. And boy was it slippery. Yes, it was an enormous eel. It was the first one Mum had ever seen in Paradise, and Dad said that he had only ever seen two others on the property. We dogs held back; Dad has warned us about snakes many times, so we were pretty wary. It certainly looked like some sort of reptile. Why, only the other evening when we were all out walking, Mum and Dad holding hands as Dad was going away to Vietnam for a couple of weeks, Dad suddenly called out really loudly to me "TRUDY, NO!" I was a bit surprised myself, because this skinny long black thing had just wriggled across my path, and I was having a good sniff. I heard Dad tell Mum afterwards that it was a poisonous red-belly black snake. Thanks, Dad, for scaring me away from it.

I might be smaller than Jessee, but I'm actually the smarter dog. One day I discovered another really weird thing. I raised the alarm and barked as loud as I could, for as long as I could. Finally Mum arrived and I showed her what I had found.

This thing was about my size, but round, and covered with huge prickles. I found this out through trial and error, as I got a bit too close in my investigation. The prickles were ever so sharp! Well, Mum called Dad and they had a conference and walked away. The next day, when I went back to visit my new acquaintance (an echidna, Mum told me), it had gone. I searched high and low, all over the garden, and finally found it down a steep wall near the edge of one of our ponds. It must have fallen in there, because no way could it have climbed down those brick walls all by itself. I don't think Mum and Dad knew what to do, so it stayed there for a few days. Eventually, Dad worked out a rescue plan. He lowered himself into the pond while Mum stood on the edge. After scooping the prickly bundle into a flower pot, he put it in a bag and handed it up to Mum.

Then we all went for a nice walk along the lake. Near the end, Dad put the bag down and turned it upside down. Now this echidna, Spike we had decided to call it, was sitting right on top of a big ants' nest. Next thing it was sending dirt flying here, there and everywhere, in all directions. And within only a few minutes, it had burrowed right into the ground and disappeared! Dad was mighty pleased, as he said ants are one of Spike's favourite foods. I've never seen any of his relatives around the place, but I'm sure I will one of these days.

We were honoured to have Pelican Pete visit us one morning. It was only a short visit, but we had great fun watching him on the lake. We all went down with Mum to have a closer look. After a while, he soared away and landed further along the lake; then he took off up into

"What's this Mum?"

^ I asked Mum, "What's this weird thing?"

the sky and circled round, watching us, for ages. Finally he sailed off to other waters. That was pretty spectacular. He's been back three times now. We really look forward to seeing him again.

Another of our happy pastimes here in Paradise is feeding the chooks, or "wooks" as Mum calls them. Most mornings we go up to the nursery first with Dad, but Mum's good and reliable, so we make sure we're back at the house pretty soon. Mum strums a tune on the compost bin, which is filled with scraps from the kitchen, and sings us a song called "The Teddy Bear's Picnic" as we set off.

A few weeks ago, we had some visitors staying in our house for a while. Dad brought home four little brown chickens and they lived in a cardboard house in the laundry. He even made them a fake Mummy – he cut one of Mum's black cotton sarongs into strips that looked just like the feathers of a chook. Each night the chickens vanished into the folds of these wings and each morning they poked their heads out to say good morning. Dad had to hold me on the edge of the box to have a look because I couldn't see over the top. I would have really liked to get closer, but he wouldn't

< We are very proud of our handsome rooster. He has a very nice personality and enjoys our daily visit.

> This chook made a lovely surrogate mother for our three new black babies but didn't really take to Dad's four little brown chickens, which is why he had to hand-raise them in the laundry.

let me! I just love chickens – they make me feel so peckish.

Now we have three black chickens as well. Jessee's big black nose pokes nearly right through the hole she has made in the wire wall of the chicken shed. And every morning we girls greet our bird friends with a bit of a rowdy chorus.

Mum wasn't too impressed one day a few years ago. She came home to find an enormous carpet snake down in the chicken house – with a big lump in the middle of it. And her favourite chicken, the prettiest one, was missing. Guess where it was!

It's all fun and games here in Paradise. Many a night there's a party held on our roof – or is it races? Dad says it's only the possums, but they haven't invited us up there yet. And one morning when we looked out the bedroom window, with Jessee holding the curtain back as she likes to do, we saw a truly wonderful sight. Mr and Mrs Duck and their eleven new babies were having breakfast on the lawn, just a few metres in front of us! They stayed around for several weeks and we had some delightful encounters with them.

Much to our delight, Pelican Pete soared high above us – up, up and away.

Our Doggy Paradise

< Our pretty new silver-laced Wyandotte called Sparkle.

> Mum and Dad take every visitor to see this bower. It's hidden away in the garden and everyone stands in awe. I don't know where the bowerbird gets his stock of blue things – pegs, pens, straws, milk container tops, you name it... He must be very, very clever.

∧ This tiny kingfisher bird is Mum's favourite. It looks like a little toy wearing a beautiful blue dress.

Many other birds visit us regularly, including graceful white egrets, heron and ibis; screeching black gang-gang cockatoos, some with striking red heads; white sulphur-crested cockatoos; cormorants and lots of moorhens and swamphens, which wander all over the place. Gorgeous kookaburras, with their unmistakeable laugh that sounds a bit like a turkey gobble gone wrong, love to perch on Mum's clothesline or on top of the barbecue house, where they can have a grand overview of what's going on. And right in front of the house, Mum has put a bird feeder, which keeps us, and our brother Paws, entertained for hours on end. Big brown doves, huge wonga pigeons, tiny finches and stunning king parrots (which are green with red heads and breasts), rainbow lorikeets and crimson and eastern rosellas all eat there contentedly, although not at the same time. I've decided that wonga pigeons must be rather clever. Once one crashed through the kitchen window behind Dad as he was talking to Mum. It made a terrific explosion and landed on the floor; there was shattered glass all over the place. We were stunned. There was a perfect hole in the window glass, and before we knew it, the pigeon had risen from the dead and flown out again through that tiny hole! Incredible! Dad said afterwards that he thought Mum must have blown up the oven with her latest cake.

Oh, I nearly forgot another activity in our busy daily lives. We dogs help Mum feed the carp in the fish pond every afternoon. It's my job to catch their attention, and I do this by barking at the very top of my lungs. Jessee and I also help Mum carry the fish pellets from the barrel where she stores them. We do this by jumping up and down all over her so that she always manages to spill a few for us on the way to the pond. We know we're very lucky to live in Paradise. I just wish we could share our home with all the other dogs in the world.

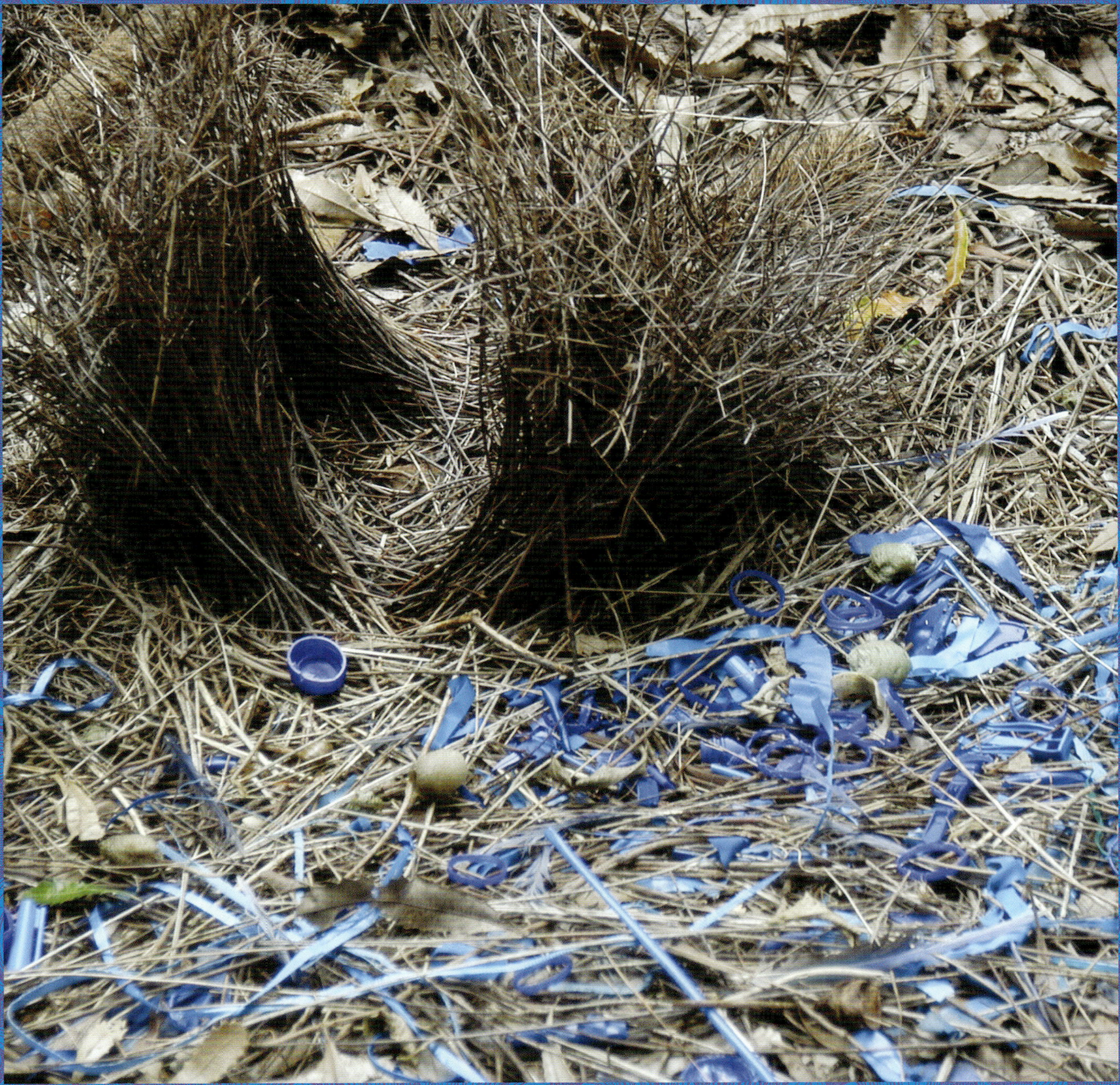

MY TRUDY

Not so long ago, I decided to rearrange the furniture in our house so that our big rectangular table had the best view. Looking out to the lake in the distance, with the bird feeder in the foreground for additional entertainment, it would then have a truly inspirational vista for writing.

On Trudy's last morning, after the dogs had eaten their breakfast, I sat down to eat my own breakfast at this long table. When I glanced to my left, I saw that Trudy was immediately outside the window, strategically situated so that she could see exactly where I was and what I was doing. "Look after your mother," were Bob's last words as he gave her a final pat and cuddle on the morning of his departure for Vietnam. The ever vigilant Trudy had taken note of his instruction and was not letting me out of her sight.

23 February 2008 was such a bright, beautiful day and Trudy, Jessee and I enjoyed several lovely walks. There was only one slight hitch, in the afternoon, when Jessee pinched Trudy's half of the lamb bone and I had to pull Trudy off her. Being the oldest – although smaller – Trudy was simply trying to assert her rights as the Boss Dog.

Just before five o'clock, I decided to eat a small goat's cheese tart for an early dinner. It was a recent experiment I had made that also included grated zucchini, red onion and thyme, and it tasted delicious. Bob had only departed for Vietnam three days before and it was a luxury for me to eat so early. Jessee and Trudy had already eaten a few frozen chicken necks each – one of their favourite meals.

I took my tart down to the end room to watch television and the dogs happily trotted along after me. Trudy strutted along, her tail held high, especially proud to be carrying out her duties as guard dog. She

"Look After Your Mother"

∧ Jessee swimming, with the fish.

jumped up into her normal position on the chaise lounge, directly facing me – just to keep an eye on my every movement. Jessee sat on the sofa with me, but Trudy was the one in charge. Little did we all know what the next hour held in store.

Sounding the Alarm

Immersed in my programme, I became aware that Trudy had been barking incessantly outside, near the house, for a while – a constant, insistent bark that always meant "Come and have a look Mum." Finally I went outside to find Trudy, who had let herself out through the doggy door earlier. She was sitting on the ground, not far from our bedroom window, looking up at a raised garden bed in which I had planted heliotrope.

    I stood next to her and wondered what was continuing to attract her attention. Then I heard a most peculiar low growl. Jessee stayed well in the background. In that corner, possums often run along the telephone cable at night, directly onto the roof of the house. Although I had never seen a possum there, I thought that perhaps Trudy could smell a baby possum. Because I could not see anything, I took another curious, but cautious, step towards the bed to peer into the foliage. Along the wall at the back, through a small gap in the foliage, I saw what I thought to be a lizard – it was brown, about 2 inches wide and quite thick. I waited a little longer, Trudy still sitting on the ground by my side, but nothing happened so then I took another final, fateful step, right into the corner to investigate further. In a lightning flash, Trudy was at my side. She had jumped up onto the garden bed

∧ "Steadfast, loyal and true."

" Trudy was a human dog "

∧ Me and Mum amongst the forget-me-nots.

and was wrestling with a snake in her mouth. It all happened so very fast. I screamed "No, Trudy!" and grabbed my precious dog. When the snake had reared to strike me, Trudy had jumped between the two of us to save my life – before I even realised what was happening.

    I carried her back inside and we settled down in front of the TV once again. Trudy seemed quite alright so I assumed she had not been bitten by the snake. But I phoned my mother just to check and she, too, thought all was OK. After about ten minutes, on my way into the kitchen, I noticed Trudy hiding under a low table and then I saw diarrhoea – and further away she had been sick. Now it was not unusual for her to be sick sometimes, but the diarrhoea was quite abnormal. I phoned our local vet but could get no answer and then I remembered our friends, Sandy and John Price, who had lost a dog from a snake bite about 12 months before – they would know the symptoms. "Get her straight to a vet," said John.

    I looked down the hallway and saw Trudy cowering at the end of it – and her normally beautiful brown eyes had turned an iridescent blue as the poison worked its way through her body. I later learnt that this was because the poison dilates the pupils, but at that time, it felt like the devil himself had taken possession of my dog. Urgent action was required, but now I was having trouble thinking clearly.

All Too Quickly

Trudy was patiently waiting for me to help her. She had moved to my study and was sitting near the window. I wrapped her in her pink towels and headed straight for the car. But instead of following the detailed instructions that John and Sandy had given me over the phone to get to the closest vet, Trudy and I went on our last trip together down the beautiful Yarramalong Valley to the only other vet

"If you had a bad day, you could rely on Trudy to come by and put the sm

> Trudy listening carefully to Bob's instructions.

I could think of by that stage. She sat peacefully on the seat next to me, facing me the whole way down – and I rested one hand on her as we comforted each other. Towards the end, just as I turned at the traffic lights at Wyong onto the old Pacific Highway, Trudy sat up and moved towards me. I know she wanted to come and sit on my lap but, through my flood of tears, I gently said no as I needed to concentrate on my driving. She had shaken off the pink towels I had wrapped her in. She made a funny little noise, then shook her head and put her paws gently over the edge of the seat. Then she flopped onto my green bag, which was on the floor, and died. She had gone just like that – and although I sensed it, I could not believe it. Only about fifty minutes had passed since she had been bitten. A few minutes later I pulled up at the veterinary clinic, which had closed; two staff members were still talking outside.

I said, "I think my dog has just died." Trudy's tongue was slightly showing, and they confirmed the worst. I then reached into the car to pick up my darling dog

ick on your face " CAROLYN STEWART

Tribute to Trudy

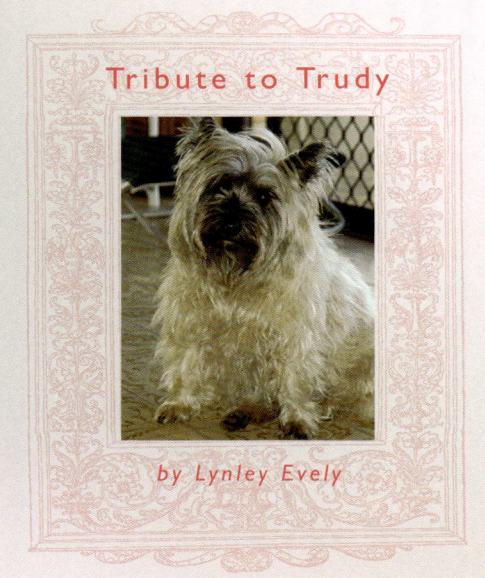

by Lynley Evely

*One who is steadfast, loyal and true
All through the years, be they many or few
One who will sit and listen to me,
Whether I speak in sadness or glee.
One who is there with a lick on the hand,
When I am nervous, or unsure of the land.
Lifts my morale when I'm weary or down,
Tells me I'm wonderful –
though I know I'm a clown.
Shares in my laughter, my joys and my tears
Steadies with wisdom all of my fears
Happily joins in a joke or two
Or any fool thing that I might do
And when I am weary at the end of the day
Shows that she loves me in her
own Trudy way.*

for the last time – her body was still warm and cuddly and her little head flopped into my neck. My grief was almost unbearable. They opened up the clinic and we laid Trudy on the bench. I could scarcely bear to leave her there. The girl from the clinic said could she phone someone and that I should not be driving. Trudy was to be frozen overnight and I would collect her in the morning to bury her at home. Next to losing my father in 1978, this was the saddest thing I have had to face in my life.

I then went down to see my mother, and later that fateful evening came home alone to cry the whole night through without sleep. Paws, our cat, put on a great display of sympathy by jumping onto the window ledge above my bed every half hour all through the night, whilst Jessee slept on top of the bed. Next morning I went down to collect Trudy with our neighbour, Sharon. On our return home, I opened the bag and hugged Trudy for the very last time. Tom, Sharon's husband, arrived to dig the hole – and Yuki, their Japanese exchange student, came too. Sandy and John turned up as well. I wrapped Trudy in her favourite pink towels and placed her in the ground that I had carefully chosen near the door of my study, so that she will always be close to me. It was one of her favourite haunts for chasing little lizards, right next to the fish pond in front of our house. I can still see her chasing them with glee over and around the rocks.

The snake was a death adder. They are often called "deaf" adders as they lie in wait and ambush their victims, unlike other snakes who slither away. They are the world's seventh deadliest snake and can change colour to camouflage themselves. If the snake had bitten me in an artery, I would have been dead within 3 minutes, and if it had bitten me elsewhere I would have died within 2 hours. Bob has never seen a death adder on our 92 hectares of lovely wooded mountainous land and I did not even know of their existence. But Ross Darby has seen one – he has since shown me the photo he took of it on the way down to the creek. If only I had known! I would have grabbed Trudy and gone straight inside.

In the days after Trudy died, Jessee kept sniffing around and looking for her everywhere. Along the banks of the lake, she ran around in circles. When I went to see what she was encircling, it was a little Trudy poo. How do you tell a dog that her best mate will never again play with her? It is so very hard for Jessee to understand what has happened.

    I held a memorial service for Trudy three weeks later, after Bob returned home. Nearly all the staff attended and signed the memorial book. Everyone misses the smiley face that brightened up their day. For me, Trudy has joined the ranks of heroic dogs, the most famous that I have ever heard of being Greyfriars Bobby. This Skye Terrier, a close relative of Cairn Terriers, lived until he was 16 years old and spent the last 14 years of his life guarding his master's grave in a cemetery in Edinburgh. The endearing statue of him in the streets of Edinburgh, which was erected in 1873, a year after his death, is a reminder of the total devotion this little dog had for its owner. My Trudy was surely a descendant of Greyfriars Bobby. One day she shall have her own statue, too.

In the Days to Follow

< This statue sits above a child's grave on the shore of Lake Maggiore in Italy. Its expression of overwhelming sadness reminds me of losing Trudy.

Our grove of *Taxodium distichum* or swamp cypress trees.

Autumn Gold

222

Our Autumn Show

There is a chill in the air and a slight frost on the ground. Autumn has arrived, but here in Paradise, instead of looking bleak and bare, our garden is springing into life as the camellias start to flower. I just popped up to the Kulnura General Store to buy extra milk for some unexpected guests and, on the way back, I saw our distinctive blue and yellow sign pointing to Paradise and felt a surge of pride. That's where I live! Tomorrow is the first day of our May open weekend. We have been making preparations for weeks and the garden is looking just right. The tents are up, the sun is shining, and, although many leaves have fallen, the garden is still glowing with the wondrous gold and red shades of autumn.

Our group of volunteers have done a splendid job with their floral displays. The amazing 85-year-old John Mathews, who also takes guided tours of the garden throughout the weekend, has worked all day on twelve magnificent arrangements; including one with autumn leaves and orange gladioli, and another exquisite arrangement of pink camellias. John has been helping out ever since our open weekends began in 1996. The industrious Barwick family, as usual, have set out all the various *Camellia* blooms with identification labels, and our ikebana enthusiasts have used all sorts of natural wonders in their ingenious creations.

< TOP L–R: The vibrant seed from the *Chamaedorea* palm, commonly known as the bamboo palm, in an arrangement by members of the Sogetsu School of Ikebana, who transform our plants during our open weekends; The lotus become dried stalks in autumn, such a contrast to their summer blooms; My favourite *Liquidambar styraciflua* tree in the whole garden. Its autumn colouring is magnificent. CENTRE L–R: Autumn is the season to rest and nest; Spectacular, but deadly poisonous, *Amanita muscaria* mushrooms often sprout up on Bunny Hill in autumn; The hollow roots of our swamp cypress are extraordinary. BOTTOM L–R: Bob loves the grey, pink and blue shades of bark on this rare tropical birch, *Betula cylindrostacys*, which grew from seed that he collected in China – its leaves turn a lovely yellow in autumn; Lichen makes an unusual feature growing on the trunk of a *Camellia*; The flower from the beautiful cycad *Cycas revoluta*, which grows near our gargoyle wall fountain.

The Season to Harvest

As this is harvest time, I have laid out all my vivid orange French pumpkins in a neat row leading to the floral display tent. I think they will be a real talking point. I have also been busy harvesting our crosses with 'Lynley's Lilac' rose. As I pick off the plump hips, I think about autumn and the changes that it brings. Some of the best hips are from crosses with the rose 'Great News', so perhaps that is an omen for the year to come. This is my first open weekend without Trudy for nearly eight years. Bob is hoping we might get a new rose from our crosses, coloured white with a lavender picotee edge. If this does eventuate, it will be named 'Trudy'.

During our open weekend last August, both dogs were with me in the top tent while I was selling plants. They had their own baskets, although they kept swapping, and at one stage I put Trudy on top of the trestle table so that she had a better view of what was going on. Every so often a little walk was necessary, which inevitably meant passing by the Gosford City Rural Fire Service stall to collect another tasty sausage.

∧ This seed from our clump of bullrush looks just like a cat's bushy tail.

∨ Autumn reflections make a tranquil scene on our lake.

Even though we have a warm semi-tropical winter climate, we have wonderful autumn colour. Bob has judiciously planted trees from his own selections, both in the wild and from our garden. One of his major joys in gardening is to grow plants from seed that he has collected – they bring back so many wonderful memories of places and people. For tree planting, his enduring motto is: "Always collect seed from the trees showing the best colour at autumn." Thanks to his careful selection, our autumn colour range is now glorious – bright yellows and oranges, rust through to scarlet and burgundy, and even some black leaves. Bob has also selected trees that drop their coloured leaves at different times, some earlier and some later in autumn, which extends the season in Paradise.

Liquidambars have the best colour range for us, especially *Liquidambar styraciflua*, commonly known as sweetgum, hailing from southern USA and the Gulf of Mexico. These trees are such a handsome shape and offer great variation within species. *Liquidambar orientalis*, from Turkey, has golden yellow foliage with an attractive incised leaf, and *Liquidambar formosanum* turns a stunning red colour later in the season. Bob finds this species especially interesting since some trees are virtually evergreen, with huge leaves. He collected seeds for our trees in south-east China, including on the island of Hainan, and in Vietnam.

Leaves of Scarlet and Gold

∧ One year our grove of Japanese *Acer palmatum* maples turned the most fantastic colours ever.

\> The luscious ripe seeds of *Michelia maudiae*

\< Trudy admiring her Mum's arrangement of berried treasure in the shape of a fan.

Liquidambar styraciflua trees are our best performers for autumn colour.

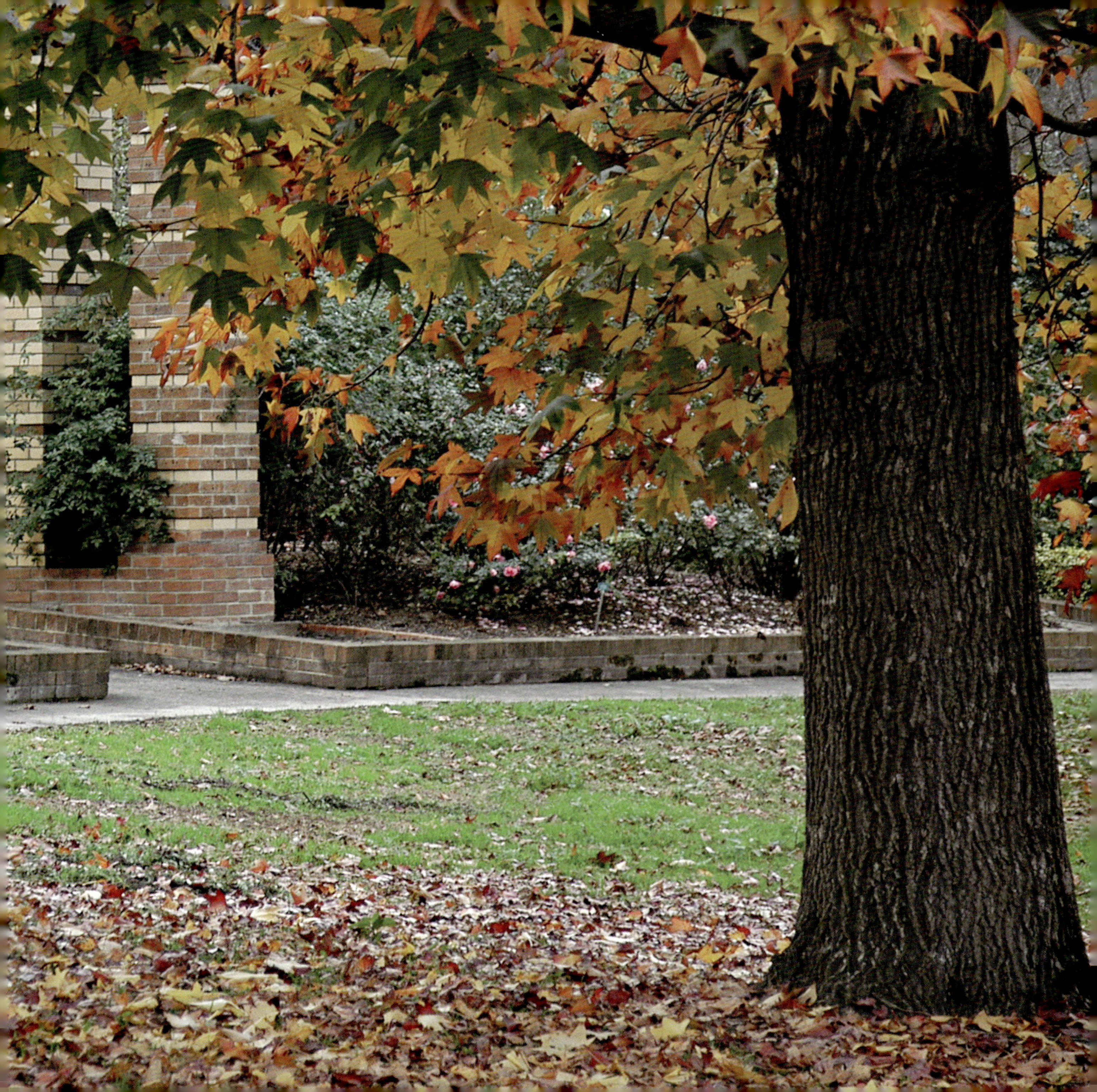

Many rare maples also grow in Paradise. The dainty-leafed Japanese variety 'Shishigashira' is my favourite, but Bob is keen on *Acer davidii* grown from seed that he collected in Yunnan. The leaves of *Acer mono* and *Acer cappadocicum* turn a deep crimson in mid-winter, and *Acer craigbei*, growing from seed that Peter Valder collected in Burma, puts on a stunning orange-red display in late autumn. It's fun collecting maple seedlings and I can still see Bob's sisters, Jan and Susie, down on their knees digging up babies to plant in their new homes in Tasmania a couple of years ago.

Other Paradise treats are the deep red colour of *Fraxinus angustifolia* 'Raywoodii' (claret ash), and our two groves of trident maple, which shade the house and make a lovely picnic setting for the staff Christmas barbecue. The seeds from these trees are encased in a dry fruit called a samara, with tiny light-green wings. They appear to hover like helicopters in the air before floating to the ground in their thousands, and growing into little seedlings scattered throughout the whole garden! And the *Nyssa* (tupelo tree) in the middle of the oval lawn near our driveway is always a star attraction with its graceful spreading branches – especially during autumn when its leaves turn a translucent apricot-orange colour with additional red tonings.

∧ Bob enjoying his evening walk under *Liquidambar styraciflua* on Bunny Hill.

> In autumn, rose hips can either be left on the bush or harvested.

> TOP L–R: This dazzling *Gladiolus* species is always used in our autumn open weekend floral display; A glorious *Liquidambar styraciflua*. BOTTOM L–R: This friendly metal frog, underneath the Japanese maple, *Acer palmatum* 'Shishigashira', heralds the arrival of guests at our front door; Stunning reflections of *Liquidambar styraciflua* and lotus on our lake.

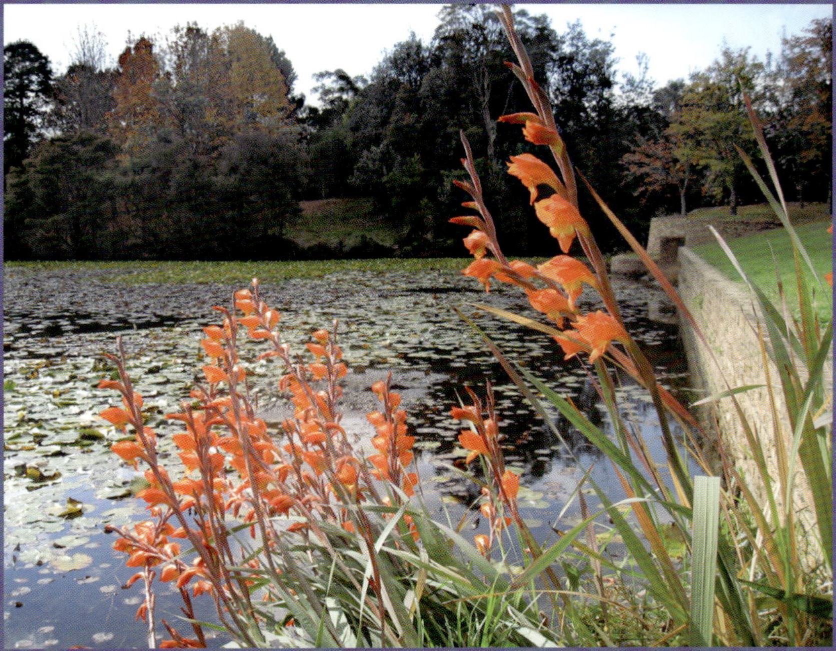
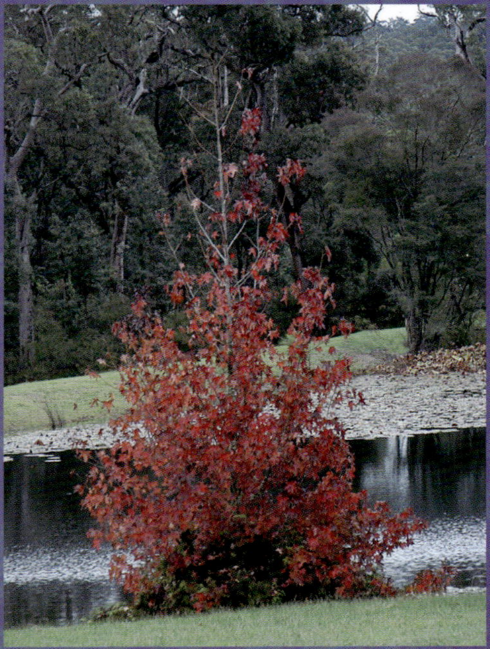
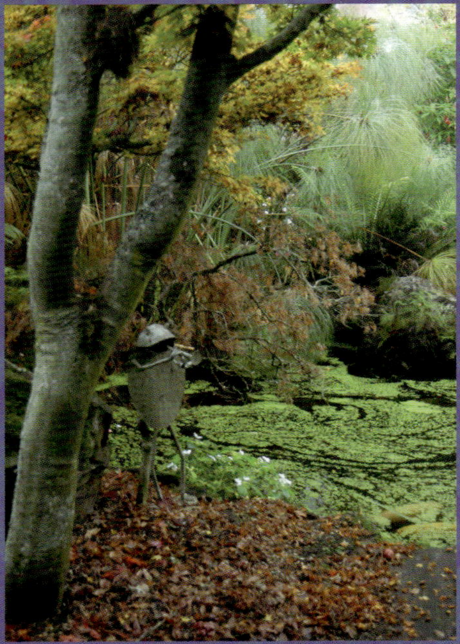
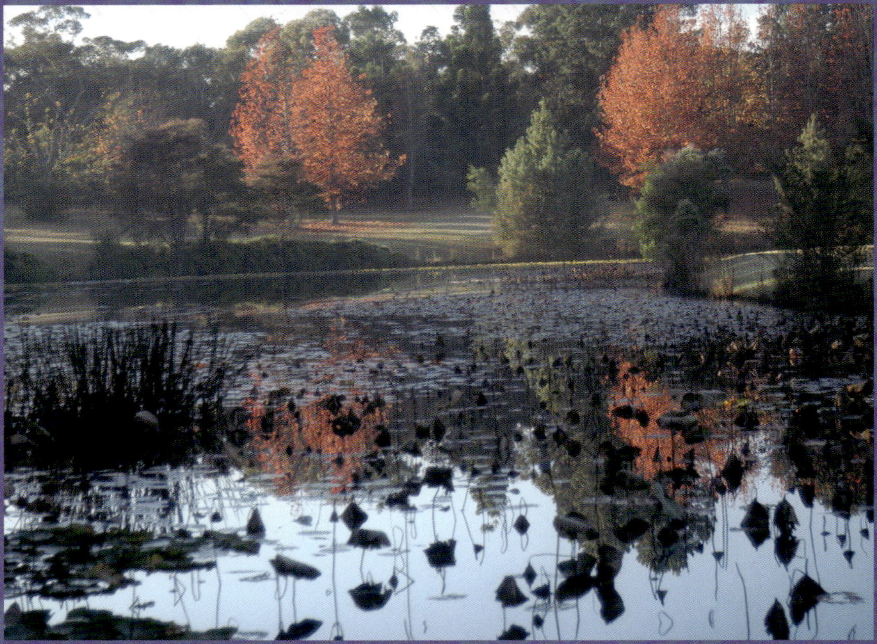

∧ The attractive seed from *Taxodium distichum* var. *ascendens*.

The most peculiar "knees" of the *Taxodium distichum* or swamp cypress.

Trees with Knees?

"Isn't it a shame that all those beautiful trees have died!" visitors sometimes comment when they see our *Taxodium distichum*, or swamp cypress trees. Originating in the swamplands of Florida's Everglades, their feather-like leaves turn a russet-brown in autumn, which is why some people think they have died. But it is their extraordinary "knees" that are their most remarkable feature. Strange hollow roots, shaped like knobbly knees, protrude through the ground underneath the branches and act like snorkles which enable the trees to breathe in their congested swampy origins. We also have *Taxodium distichum* var. *ascendens*, a slender form of the swamp cypress that grows no wider than 2 metres. And a Chinese water cypress, *Glyptostrobus*, has a special place in our garden; it is nearly extinct in the wild. With so many rarities and delights to discover, our Paradise is a plant collector's heaven.

Bob is especially proud of his *Metasequoia glyptostroboides*. This stately cone-shaped tree, named in Chinese "water fir" or "water larch", was thought to be extinct until trees were discovered growing in China in 1946. From these humble beginnings, much like the Wollemi pine, it is now growing in thousands of gardens throughout the world. Several years ago, when we met with a group of tree lovers in northern New South Wales for a few days, Bob again showed his prowess in discovering plants. This time, it was ancient *Ginkgo* and cycad fossils embedded in rock: the very first one he chose to split open was a perfect example, so much so that the palaeontologist leading the excursion asked to keep it, to take to a museum.

∧ Jessee on an evening walk in autumn, sadly now without her best friend Trudy.

Whatever the season, the sunsets in Paradise are superb.

As our May 2008 autumn open weekend draws to a close, I think about all the visitors who came to our garden for the first time. They were thrilled to discover a little touch of paradise near Sydney and can't wait for the spring riot of colour during our next open weekend in August. Only ten days now before Bob and I fly off to Europe. We will be away for two months. Trudy always hated us leaving and, on one occasion, she even jumped into my suitcase as I was packing. Annie, Trudy's special mate in the nursery, recounts how she would sit in the middle of the road patiently waiting for our return. And lift her head in anticipation every time a car arrived. I can see her still, every time I turn into the driveway. As soon as she and Jessee heard my car, they would rush off and wait for me just at the entrance – and then come bounding after my car with glee. When I opened the door, Trudy was always the first to greet me.

And so I go to bed and dream of plants, dogs and aeroplanes. Bob has promised that when we return we will get two new Cairn Terrier puppies, or possibly even a West Highland White Terrier and a Cairn Terrier. We have already chosen their names: Misty, and Trudy 3.

Dogs of the Future

∧ An amazing transformation from exquisite flower to seed pod takes place in this *Camellia gigantocarpa* species. The pods are more than 7 cm in diameter.

> *"Gather ye rosebuds while ye may,*
> *Old Time is still a-flying:*
> *And this same flower that smiles to-day,*
> *To-morrow will be dying."*
>
> ROBERT HERRICK 1591–1674

Striped camellias, such as 'Jean Lyne', often produce many different coloured flowers on the same bush.

Acknowledgements

First and foremost, thanks to my husband for making the Paradise in which we live. I am glad we found each other at the Melbourne International Flower Show. Thanks too to the two people who have worked with me in producing this book. Firstly my brilliant editor, Catherine Page, whose diligence and discerning eye has helped on countless occasions throughout the whole production. And thanks to Di Quick. So many times, when she was my colleague in publishing, I admired her designs. Now she has transformed my photos and text, with her inimitable style, into a book which truly delights me. I consider her one of Australia's best designers – if not the best.

And multiple thanks to Leo Schofield, for writing the foreword to my book – the garden you created at Bronte House has been a source of inspiration for both of us. Sincere gratitude also for the input from two marvellous and extremely knowledgeable plant enthusiasts, Rosemary and Maurice Foster. Finally, thanks to my beautiful mother, who has stood by me and guided me all through my life's journey. Not forgetting, of course, Trudy and Jessee, the first two dogs that I have ever owned; they form such an integral part of this book.

The lemon shades of 'Teasing Georgia' in the foreground blend well in this bed near our oval lawn.

Index

[page numbers in *italics* refer to illustrations and captions]

Aboriginal relics 123
Acer 225, 228, *229*
Agapanthus 141, *141*
Alstromeria 190
Alyssum 104–5, 191, *191*
Amaranthus 143
Amaryllis belladonna 133, 138, *138*
annuals 187–93
anthill 122
Aquilegia 187
architectural design 71
Arctotis 188
Argyranthemum 96
aster 197
August (spring) open weekend 43, 96, 139, 224, 233
Austin, David 155, 180
Australian Quarantine and Inspection Service 92
autumn 221–33
autumn colour 225–28
autumn (May) open weekend 43, 223–24, 233
azaleas 197

bandstand 67
bangalow palm 131
barbecue house 73
bay trees 114, *114*
beans 111, *111*
Begonia 43, 116
belladonna lilies 138
belvedere 71, 77
berries 225
Better Homes and Gardens 99
Bidens 189
birch 222
bird of paradise 142, *142*
birds 209–12
Bloodtree Festival 112
Blue Mountains Rhododendron Garden 197
bluebells 81
bonsai 88
Boronia 131
botanising 79–93
"Bottle, The" 164
bowerbird 213
Brazil 137
breeding plants 27, 45
  Camellia sasanqua 19–21
  polyanthus 40
brickwork 65–66, *64–77*
bridges *3*, 64–65, *64–65*, 81, *89*
Buddha's Hand *117*
Buddleia 57, *57*

bullrush 224
Bunny Hill 201–6
Bunya pines 120
bush 118–30, *120–27*
bushfire 126–27

cabbages 108
Cairn Terriers 45, 233
Calkin, Robert 155
Camellia 12–31, 84–85, 223
  azalea (syn. *changii*) 22, *22*
  gigantocarpa 233
  hybrids 16, 18–19, 23, 24, 26, 27, *27*, 29, 35
  japonica 17–18, *18*, 19, 21–22, 30, 234
  longipedicellata 23
  pitardii var. *pitardii* 13
  reticulata 12, 15, 18, 19, 26, 28, 30, 90
  sasanqua 19–21, *20–21*, 23–27, *26*, 29, 31
  sinensis 15, *17*
  williamsii 24
Camellia cultivars
  'Captain Rawes' 19
  'Chuxiong Gold' 15, 18
  'Contemplation' 16, 29
  'Dr Clifford Parks' 28
  'Dream Boat' 19

'Dream Girl' 27
'Eighteen Scholars' 28
'Flower Girl' 26, 27, *27*
'Incarnata' 17–18, *18*
'Jean Lyne' 234
'Jouvan' 30
'Lasca Beauty' 28, 30
'Paradise Elizabeth' 31
'Paradise Illumination' 35
'Paradise Jessica' 31
'Paradise Joy' 31
'Paradise Little Miss E' 23, 24
'Paradise Pearl' 21
'Paradise Petite' 26
'Paradise Rebecca' 31
'Paradise Regina' 23, 25
'Paradise Sayaka' 21
'Purple Gown' 15
'R. L. Wheeler' 22
'Raspberry Glow' 26
'Red Willow' 20
'Roma Risorta' 21
'Shishigashira' 24, 26
Show Girl 27, *27*
'Sparkling Burgundy' 24, 29
'Temple Mist' 12
'Water Lily' 18–19
'Wynne Raynor' 24
Cardiocrinum giganteum var. *yunnanense* 78

Cedar Park Lavender Farm 38
Ceratopetalum gummiferum see Christmas bush
cherries 155
cherry blossom 90, 94–101, 96–99, 107
chickens 210–11, 210–11
China 14, 15, 17–18, 28, 81–90, 83, 86–92, 134, 143
Christmas bush 118, 120, 123
chrysanthemums 91
church window 73, 94, 99
Chuxiong 18
cineraria 42–43
Clark, Alister 180–81
Cochrane, Trevor 116
coleus 42
collecting *see* plant collecting
Cosmos 187, 191
"crazy wall" 66, 67, 70
creeks 124–25, 128–29
Cuphea 84
cuttings, growing roses from 173
cycads 131, 223, 231
Cymbidium 138–39, 139

Dahlia 184, 196
daphne 57
dead-heading roses 146, 180
death adders 218–19
decorated saucers 191

Delbard roses 155, 156, 167
diamond python 206, 206–7
Dianthus 27, 59–60, 60–61, 149
Doryanthes 120, 123
ducks 124, 211
Duncan, Walter 151–53, 163

echidna 209, 209
eels 208, 208
"Eiffel Tower" 71, 76
Elizabeth Bay House 180–81
Engelhardtia spicata 82
Epacris longiflora 123
Evely, Lynley 168, 218

FAO code of conduct 92
fire 126–27
fish pond 212
fleur-de-lys 140
"flower lady" 198–99, 198
follies 63–77
forget-me-nots 189, 216
fossils 231
fountain 67, 74–75
fragrance 47–61, 155
frangipani 55–56
Fraxinus 221, 228
frogs 125, 229

Gardenia 55, 55, 130
gargoyles 67, 74–75
Gawler Sweet Peas 49

geebung 120–23
Gladiolus 229
Glenara 181
Glyptostrobus 231
goannas 207
Gordonia 90, 90
Great Dixter 186
Greek columns 66, 68–69
Greyfriars Bobby 219
Griggs, Johanna 99
grotto 73
Guillot roses 150–54, 151–55
gum
  red-flowering 120–22
  scribbly 203, 204
Gymea lilies (*Doryanthes*) 120, 123
Gypsophila 162, 162

Hampton Court Palace Flower Show 92
harvest time 224
Hedychium coccineum 115
Heliotropum arborescens 56, 56
Heritage Garden, The 150–51, 152
Hever Castle 180
Hibiscus 143, 142–43
hollyhocks 187
hydrangeas 34, 36–38, 37, 39, 90, 120

ikebana 142, 222, 223
irises 140–41, 142–43

Jacaranda 104, 105
Jessee 44, 45, 67, 124, 125, 189, 207, 214, 219

Kanding 86, 87–89, 87, 89
King's Garden 77, 157
kingfisher 212
kookaburras 212
Kulnura Garden Club 54, 135

Lady's Slipper 194
lake 2–3, 73, 203, 224
larkspurs 147, 149, 150, 186, 187
lavender 44, 44–45, 85, 85, 87
Lepidozamia 131
lilac 53–54, 54, 57
Linaria 187
lions 71
Liquidambar
  formosanum 225
  orientalis 225
  styraciflua 223, 225, 226–29
lizards 147, 181, 207
Lloyd, Christopher 186, 195
Lobelia 149, 197, 197
lotus 134–35, 134–35, 222, 228, 229
Luculia 52, 52, 55
lyrebird 207

Macleay, Alexander 180–81
Macoboy, Stirling 55
Magnolia 97, 102–5, 102–5

campbellii 105
denudata 104–5
'San Jose' 102, *102*, *104*
'Starwars' 102, *102*
Mangrove Mountain Country Fair 191
maples 225, 228, *229*
Marguerite daisy *96*
Mathews, John 223
Matilda poppies *4*, 28–30, *43*
May bush *95*, 105, 106–7
May (autumn) open weekend 43, 223–24, 233
Melbourne International Flower Show 30, 156
Metasequoia glyptostroboides 231
Michelia maudiae 225
Monet, Claude 135
"monkey colony" 70, *72*, *187*
mulching 111
mushrooms *207*, 222

Nambour Flower Show 38
nasturtiums *117*
New Guinea 142
Nicholson, Howard 116–17, *117*
Nieuwesteeg, John 165
nursery 35–45
Nyssa 228

obelisk *73*, 76
observatory *71*, *73*, *97*
open weekends 43

orchids 85–87, *122*, 123, *138*–*39*, 139
Osmanthus delavayi 56, *56*

pansies 49, 187, 191, *194*–*95*
Paradise (garden) 10–11
Paradise Plants (nursery) 35–45
Parks, Dr Clifford 28
Paws (cat) *182*, *212*
Paxton, Joseph 136
Pelargonium 186
Pelican Pete 209–10, *211*
perfume 47–61, 155
Persoonia 120–23
Petunia 189, *193*
Phlox *193*, *198*
photinias 38
plant breeding 19–21, 27, 40, 45
plant collecting 81–92
Plumbago *185*, 191
Plumeria (frangipani) 55–56, *56*
polyanthus 36, 38, 40–43, *40*–*42*
poppies *4*, 28–30, *43*, 84
Portugal 85, 86, 87
possums *211*, *215*
preserving flowers 147
Primula 42, *98*, 187
Prunus 107
  × 'Blireiana' *99*, 99, 105, *107*
  cerasoides var. *rubea* 107
  glandulosa 'Rosea Plena' 105, *107*

hybrid 'Louise Audrey' *97*, 107
persica 'Versicolor' 107
see also cherry blossom; May bush
pumpkins 109, *112*, *113*
Pyracantha 88

"Queen's Garden" 172
"Quest for the Rose, The" 87

rabbits 203
rainforest 130–31
"Rapunzel's Tower" 71
Renmark Rose Festival 182–83, *182*–*83*
rhododendrons 90
Rix, Martyn 87–89
Roman baths 114–15, *114*
Roman bridge 64–65, *64*, *65*
Rome *93*, 114, 114–15, 146–47
rooster *210*
Rosa 87–89, 144–83, *196*
  banksiae 155, 158–59
  canina 147
  moyesii 89, *89*
Rosaceae family 155
rose cultivars
  'Abraham Darby' 174
  'Albertine' 159
  'Apricot Nectar' *166*, *167*, 169
  'Ashram' 174
  'Baroque' 174

'Bazaar' 147
'Belle Story' 174, *175*
'Bloomfield Abundance' 174
'Blossomtime' 157, *157*, 158
'Bonica' 146, *154*, 159, 162, *163*, 165, *165*, 183, *183*
'Bordure Magenta' 174
'Brass Band' 174
'Cécile Brunner' 158
'Celina' 180
'Centenaire de Lourdes' *154*–*55*, 156, 158
'Chantal Merieux' *6*, *154*
'Charles de Gaulle' *144*, 146, 174
'Chartreuse de Parme' 174
'Chicago Peace' 174
'China Doll' *164*, 165–66, *166*, *167*
'Citron Fraise' *155*
'Crepuscule' 174
'Deep Secret' 180
'Elina' 174
'Emilien Guillot' *6*
'Europeana' 174
'Fairy, The' 158, 162–65, *164*
'Fiona's Wish' *144*, 174, *175*
'Fisherman's Friend' *148*, 174
'François Juranville' 174, *176*
rose cultivars *continued*
'Gertrude Jekyll' *175*
'Golden Fairytale' *175*

Grafton Pink *156, 157, 173*
'Graham Thomas' 175, *175*
'Granada' 175
'Grand Siècle' 175
'Henri Matisse' *155*
'Home and Garden' 175
'Iceberg' 166, *169*, 183
'Kardinal' 176
'Laure Davoust' *156*
'Lavender Dream' *168, 169*
'Lavender Mist' 176
'Le Vésuve' *175*, 176
'Lovely Fairy' 165, *169*
'Lynley's Lilac' 168, *168*, 224
'Manita' 176
'Mary Rose' 176
'Megan Louise' 148
'Mister Lincoln' *144*, 146
'Molineux' 176
'Monsieur Tillier' 176
'My Choice' 177
'Nahema' 156
'Nana Mouskouri' 177
'Olde Fragrance' *175*, 177
'Paradise' 146, *158*, 181
'Pat Austin' 177, *177*
'Paul Bocuse' 153, *153*
'Perfume Delight' 177
'Pinkie' 148–49
'Portrait' 177
'Princesse de Monaco' 162
'Raymond Privat' *156*, 157
'Red Pierre' 177
'Renae' 177, *178*

'Rhapsody in Blue' 177, *177*
'Roundelay' 146, 177
'Savoy Hotel' 148, 177
'Simply Magic' 145, *146, 147, 183*
'Sonia Rykiel' 153
'Spring Song' 162, *162, 163*
'Squatter's Dream' 180
'Super Fairy' 165
'Swan' 178, *179*
'Sympathie' 177
'Teasing Georgia' 178, *179, 235*
'Tess of the D'Urbervilles' 178
'The Children's Rose' 148, *178*
'Traviata' 179
'Twilight Glow' 159
'Valencia' 179
'Versicolor' 182
'Versigny' *150*
'Victoria's Gold' 148
'Violina' 148, *179*
'William Christie' 153
'Winchester Cathedral' 179, *179*
'Zephirine Drouhin' 157
rosemary *114*
Roseraie Val-de-Marne 156, *160–61*
roses 87–89, 144–83, *196*
  cross-pollinating 168–69
  growing from cuttings 173

growing from seed 166–67
Ross, Graham 99
Ruston, David 182, *182*

samara 228
Scabiosa 195
scents 47–61, 155
Schofield, Leo 9, 137
Seale, Allan 28
seed
  growing roses from 166–67
  self-sown (annuals) 188–89
snakes 206, *206–7, 208*, 211, 215–19
snapdragons 189, *193*
Spain 80, 84–85
sports 166
spring 95–105
spring (August) open weekend 43, 96, 139, 224, 233
"Stairway to Heaven" 65, 67, 114
steel structures 71
stock 50–51, *51–52*, 53
stonework 63–77, *62–67, 70–72*, 80
Strelitzia nicholai 142, *142*
sugar cane mulch 111
swamp cypress 220, *222, 230, 231*
sweet peas 46–50, *47–51*
sweet William 59
Syringa 54
Taxodium distichum 220, *222,*

230, 231, 231
"Teddy Bears' Picnic" 72
tortoises 202, *203*
Tradescantia 197
troll 62
Trudy 5, 45, 111, *124*, 150–51, *181, 189*, 202–19, *224*, 233

vases 146, *147–48*, 193
vegetables 108–13, *110–17*
Venice 80, *81, 142*
Verbena 197, *199*
Vietnam 80, *82*
Vinca 197
violas 149, 187, 191, *192*

"wall flower" 72
wallaby 200, *202*
waratahs 120, *130*
water lilies 132, *135–36, 135–36*
water recycling 67, 73, 99
wattle 119, *125*
Welsh, Eric 148
Wisteria 47, *58–59, '59, 66–67*
Wollemi pine 130
wombats 203–6, *203*
wonga pigeons 212
Worsleya 139, *139*
Wyandotte chickens 112, *211*

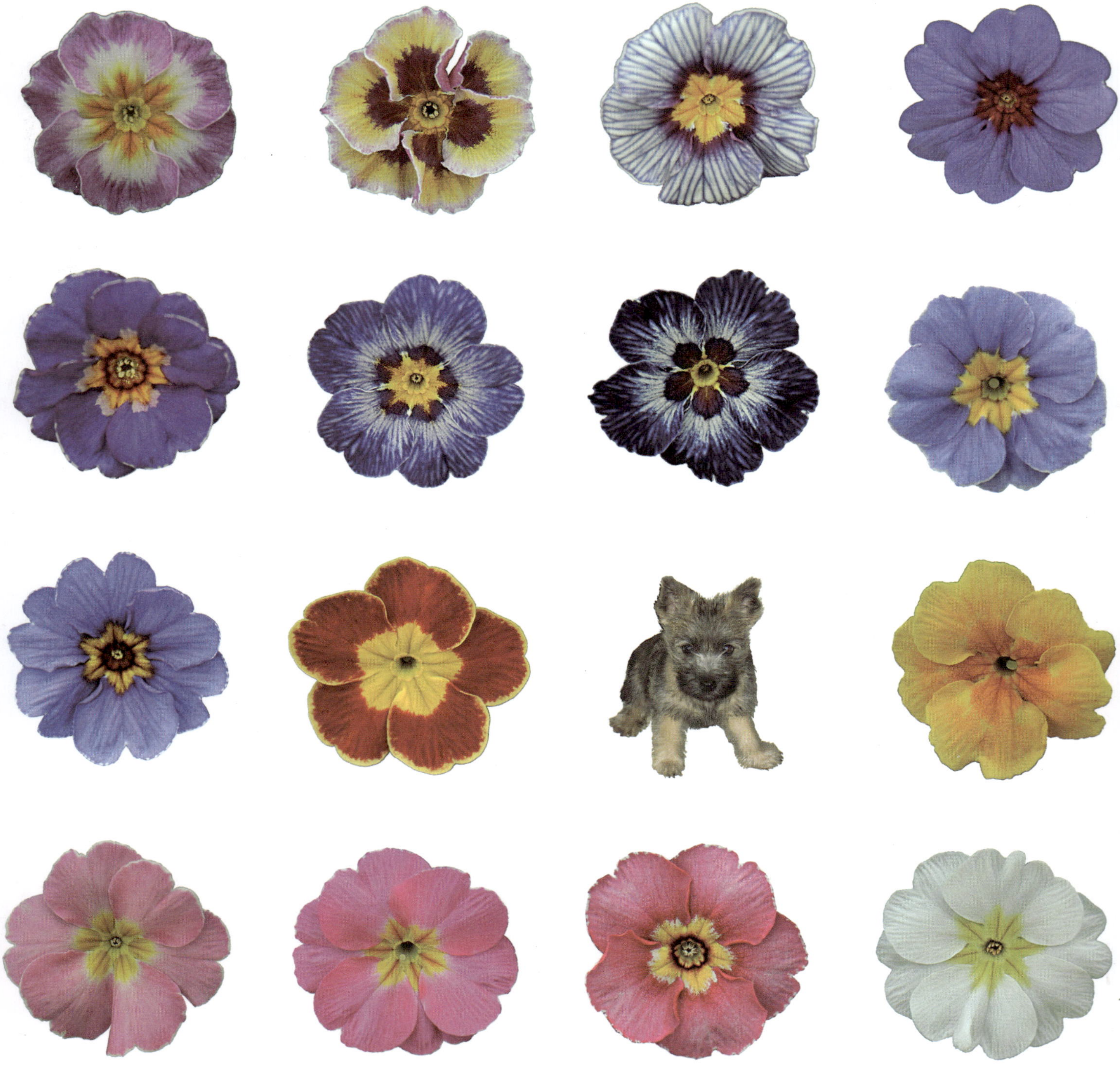